Hearts of Valor - Faithful in the Call

Joshua Rhoades

Published by Joshua Paul Rhoades, 2024.

While every precaution has been taken in the preparation of this book, the publisher assumes no responsibility for errors or omissions, or for damages resulting from the use of the information contained herein.

HEARTS OF VALOR - FAITHFUL IN THE CALL

First edition. November 25, 2024.

Copyright © 2024 Joshua Rhoades.

ISBN: 979-8230802969

Written by Joshua Rhoades.

Also by Joshua Rhoades

Courage Under Fire: David's Stand On The Battlefield
Jonah's Journey: Voices Of Redemption And Lessons In Obedience
The Furnace Of Faith: 12 Principles From The Heat Of Faith
Whispers of Hope: Inspiring Stories of Men's Prayers In Scripture
Frontier Legends: The Oregon Dream
Elijah: A Beacon Of Boldness
HOOK, LINE & SAVIOUR - Faith Reflections from Fishing
Driven By Faith: Motor Racing Inspired Christian Life
30 Day Devotional - Bold and Strong- Coffee Devotions for a Courageous Christian Walk
Authentic Christianity: The Heart of Old Time Religion
Consider The Ant - God's Tiny Preachers
Flee Fornication: The Plea For Purity
Renewed Hope- How to Find Encouragement in God
Sounding The Call - The Voice of Conviction
The Altar - Where Heaven Meets Earth
The Bible's Battlefields- Timeless Lessons from Ancient Wars
The Sacred Art of Silence - How Silence Speaks in Scripture
Under Fire- The Sanctity of the Traditional Biblical Home
Who Is on the Lord's Side? A Call to Righteousness
What Is Truth? - From Skepticism to Submission
First and Goal- Faith and Football Fundamentals
From Dugout to Devotion- Spiritual Lessons from Baseball
Par for the Course- Faith and Fairways
The Believer's Pace- Tools for Running Life's Marathon
The Immutable Fortress- Security in God's Unchanging Nature
Biblical Bravery
Deer Stands and Devotions: A Hunter's Walk with God

Jesus Knows- Our Hearts, Our Responsibility
Restoration - Setting The Bone
Spiritual 911- God's Word for Life's Emergency's
The Freedom of Forgiveness
The Jezebel Effect - Ancient Manipulations Modern Lessons
The Shout That Stopped The Saviour
The Time Machine Chronicles: Old Testament Characters
Anchored In Truth Exploring The Depths of Psalm 119
Biblical Counsel on Anger
Proverbs' Portraits The Men God Mentions
Stumbling in the Dark - The Dangers of Alcohol
Guarding the Wicket Protecting Your Faith and Game
The Champion's Faith - Wrestling and Achieving Spiritual Victory
Scriptural Commands for Modern Times Living God's Word Today Volume 1
Scriptural Commands for Modern Times Living God's Word Today Volume 2
Scriptural Commands for Modern Times Living God's Word Today Volume 3
The Greatest Gift
A Christmas Journey of Faith
Daughter Of The King: Embracing Your Identity In Christ
Determination and Dedication Building Strong Faith As A Young Man
Walking Through Walls God's Power to Part the Storms of Life
David's Song Of Deliverance Praising God Through Every Storm
From Weakness to Warrior: Gideon's Transformation
Why Did Jesus Weep?
Living For God The Call To Be A Living Sacrifice
My Mind Is In A Fog What Do I Do?
Turning The Page Written By Grace
The Calling and Greatness of John the Baptist
For Such a Time Esther's Courageous Stand
From Brokenness To Beauty Written By The Pen of Grace
The Ultimate Guide to Massive Action- From Plans to Reality
A Heart Of Conviction
Serving In The Shadows
Repentance Revealed The Road Back To God
The Chief Sinner Meets The Chief Saviour Reflections On I Timothy 1:15

Answer The Call - 31 Days of Biblical Action
The Birthmark of the Believer
Reflections on Calvary's Cross
The Kingdom Builder Paul's Bold Proclamation of Christ
The Animal Of Pride
The Reach That Restores Christ Love For The Broken
Paul- The Many Roles of a Servant of Christ
Unshakeable Faith- 31 Days of Peace in God's Word
O Come, Let Us Adore Him- A Christmas Devotional
The Shepherd's Voice
The Trail From Vision To Mission
Enabled- Living God's Purpose With Power
Held Back But Not Defeated
The Enoch Walk
The Power and Precision of God's Word
The Children Who Found Christmas
Hearts of Valor - Faithful in the Call
Why It Matters- Finding Hope in Moments of Frustration"

Dedication

To the brave and faithful,

This book is for you—the law enforcement officer who faces the unknown with courage, resilience, and unwavering determination. For the one who wears the badge with honor, shouldering the weight of responsibility and walking a path that is both demanding and sacred. For the one who answers the call to serve and protect, no matter the risk or sacrifice.

You know the meaning of sacrifice. You've endured long nights, uncertain days, and decisions made in an instant that linger in your heart. You've shown courage and compassion in moments that demanded more than strength. And even when the burden seemed overwhelming, you remained faithful—not because it was easy, but because it's who you are.

This book is for those who've faced heartbreak yet stood strong for others. For those who've been misunderstood, criticized, and overlooked but continued to serve with dignity. For those carrying unseen burdens, bearing the cost of peace and safety for others.

You are not alone. God walks beside you, sees your tears, hears your prayers, and knows the weight you carry. His strength is your anchor when you feel weak, His presence your shield when the badge feels too heavy.

Take heart. Your work matters. Your sacrifices echo in eternity. You serve with valor, guided by faith and upheld by the God who called you to this mission. May these pages remind you of His grace, love, and unshakable promises.

Thank you for your service, courage, and faithfulness. You are deeply loved, eternally valued, and never forgotten by the One who holds you in His care.

With all my heart, this is for you.

"To the brave hearts who step into the unknown with courage, compassion, and unwavering faith—may you find strength in the LORD God who called you, peace in His promises, and hope in His unfailing love."

Introduction

Day 1 - Protecting the Innocent
Day 2 - Perseverance in Duty
Day 3 - Patience Under Pressure
Day 4 - Prepared for Every Situation
Day 5 - Power of Authority
Day 6 - Pride in Service
Day 7 - Protecting Boundaries
Day 8 - Pursuing Truth
Day 9 - Peace Amidst Chaos
Day 10 - Partnering with Others
Day 11 - Perception and Discernment
Day 12 - Praising God in Success
Day 13 - Patrolling with Purpose
Day 14 - Protection from Evil
Day 15 - Provision in Need
Day 16 - Purity of Heart
Day 17 - Pardon and Forgiveness
Day 18 - Preparedness for Action
Day 19 - Persistence in Justice
Day 20 - Patience with Others
Day 21 - Promoting Peace
Day 22 - Protection through Prayer
Day 23 - Power of Compassion
Day 24 - Preventing Harm
Day 25 - Provision of Comfort
Day 26 - Protection of the Vulnerable
Day 27 - Perseverance in the Face of Danger

Day 28 - Power of God's Word
Day 29 - Putting Others First
Day 30 - Presence of God in Every Situation
Day 31 - Praise for God's Faithfulness
Conclusion

Introduction

In the life of a law enforcement officer, every shift begins with the unknown—an unpredictable world filled with challenges, risks, and moments that demand strength, courage, and resilience. Yet, amid the flashing lights, the hurried calls for help, and the weight of the badge, there lies a deeper purpose: a calling to serve, protect, and stand in the gap for others. "Hearts of Valor - Faithful in the Call" is a devotional journey crafted specifically for those who dedicate their lives to this noble mission, providing spiritual strength, encouragement, and renewal for the unique challenges faced by the law enforcement community. Each day, this 31-day devotional draws you closer to the One who called you to this service, offering God's Word as a source of wisdom, courage, and peace. Whether you're walking through moments of triumph or feeling the strain of sacrifice, this book reminds you that you are not alone; God is with you in every step, every decision, and every challenge. It reminds you that your role is not merely a job, but a divine calling—a testament to God's work through you as a guardian of peace and justice. You'll explore how to wear the full armor of God (Ephesians 6:10-18), stand firm in integrity (Proverbs 10:9), and lean on His unshakable promises even in the darkest of times (Isaiah 41:10). This devotional is more than words on a page; it's a lifeline for moments when the weight of the badge feels too heavy and a celebration of the light you shine in a world that desperately needs it. With each passing day, you'll gain practical tools for prayer, find strength in God's truth, and discover the peace that comes from knowing you serve under the Ultimate Commander. Whether you are a seasoned officer, a rookie just starting out, or someone who supports law enforcement, "Hearts of Valor - Faithful in the Call" will inspire you to live courageously, lead humbly, and serve faithfully, knowing that your work is not in vain. As you embark on this journey, may you find that God's grace is sufficient, His love is unfailing, and His presence is your greatest shield.

Take heart, for you are not alone—you serve with valor, guided by faith, and strengthened by the One who called you to this mission.

Day 1 - Protecting the Innocent

Protecting the innocent is a sacred calling, one that resonates deeply with the very heart of God. In Matthew 5:9, Jesus says, "Blessed are the peacemakers: for they shall be called the children of God." These words, simple yet profound, serve as a powerful reminder that those who work to protect and preserve peace reflect the character of God Himself. For law enforcement officers, this calling takes on an even greater weight, as their daily lives revolve around standing in the gap for those who are vulnerable, frightened, or unable to defend themselves. It's a role that demands courage, strength, and an unshakable sense of purpose, yet it also requires a heart grounded in compassion and justice. In a world that often feels chaotic and broken, the act of protecting the innocent is more than a duty—it is a ministry of love and a reflection of God's unchanging character. Officers are called to step into situations others flee from, to bring calm where there is fear, and to ensure that those who cannot protect themselves are shielded from harm. This mirrors the way Jesus lived, walking among the people, extending His hand to the marginalized, and standing against injustice. When officers respond to a child in need, comfort someone in distress, or intervene in dangerous circumstances, they embody the spirit of peacemaking that Jesus speaks of in this verse. But protecting the innocent is not without its challenges. It often requires stepping into the unknown, making split-second decisions, and facing circumstances that are emotionally and physically draining. It requires a heart that is strong yet tender, brave yet humble, and steadfast in its commitment to do what is right. This balance is not easy, and it's here that the promise of Matthew 5:9 becomes a source of strength and encouragement. Jesus's blessing on peacemakers is not only a recognition of their work but also a reminder that they are never alone in their calling. Just as officers protect the innocent, Jesus calls all His followers to protect peace and seek justice. This means living with integrity, showing kindness even in the face of hostility, and standing firm for what is right even when it is difficult. It's a calling that transcends personal gain, requiring a heart that is focused on the well-being of others and guided by God's wisdom. Protecting the innocent also reflects the ministry of Jesus, who throughout His time on earth, stood up for those who were vulnerable and defended those who were wronged. From His encounter with the woman caught in adultery to His care for the sick and marginalized, Jesus demonstrated that true justice is always rooted in love. For law enforcement officers, this means recognizing that their role is not just about enforcing the law but also about showing compassion and mercy where it is needed most. Protecting the innocent is about more than shielding people from physical harm—it is about creating a space where peace can flourish, where trust can be restored, and where communities can thrive. It is about being a beacon of light in a world that can often feel dark and overwhelming. Officers who embrace this calling do more than carry out their duties; they bring hope to those who need it most. This work can be exhausting, both physically and emotionally. Officers often carry the weight of the stories they encounter—the pain of those they have helped, the struggles of those they couldn't reach in time, and the unrelenting challenges of standing in the gap day after day. But Jesus's words remind us that this work is not in vain. Peacemakers are blessed because they align themselves with the very mission of God, and they are called His children because their actions reflect His heart. In the quiet moments, when the weight of the badge feels heavy, the promise of Matthew 5:9 can be a source of renewal and strength. It serves as a reminder that peacemaking is not just a profession but a divine calling, one that carries eternal significance. To protect the innocent is to stand as a guardian of God's justice, to bring peace into places of conflict, and to reflect the light of Christ in every interaction. It is a role that requires faith, perseverance, and a deep reliance on God's guidance. But for those who take up this mantle, there is the assurance that their work is seen, valued, and blessed by the One who called them. As Jesus said, "Blessed are the peacemakers," and this blessing is a promise that echoes through every act of protection, every moment of service, and every step taken to defend those who cannot defend themselves.

Day 2 - Perseverance in Duty

Perseverance in duty is one of the most challenging yet rewarding callings, a testament to the strength and resilience of those who serve. For law enforcement officers, the demands of their work often stretch beyond physical endurance, requiring mental toughness, emotional steadiness, and unwavering commitment. Day after day, shift after shift, they respond to calls, face uncertainty, and carry the weight of responsibility for the safety and well-being of their communities. This is not a profession for the faint of heart—it requires a unique blend of courage and compassion, strength and sacrifice. In Galatians 6:9, the Apostle Paul encourages believers with these words: "Let us not be weary in well doing: for in due season we shall reap." This verse speaks directly to the heart of perseverance, reminding us that the work we do, though difficult and sometimes unseen, is meaningful and fruitful in God's timing. Law enforcement officers embody this spirit of perseverance as they push through long hours, navigate high-pressure situations, and continue to serve even when the world feels ungrateful or indifferent. Yet, this call to persevere is not exclusive to officers. All of us, as followers of Christ, are called to serve others, to endure in the face of adversity, and to remain faithful to the tasks God has placed before us. Perseverance is about more than just completing a job—it's about honoring God through steadfastness, finding purpose in the mundane, and trusting that our efforts will bear fruit even if we don't see it right away.

For officers, perseverance often means showing up, day after day, even when the job feels thankless or overwhelming. It means running toward danger when others run away, answering every call for help with the same sense of urgency, and standing firm in moments of chaos. It means staying focused during the long, lonely hours of a night shift and maintaining integrity when no one is watching. These acts of perseverance, though exhausting, reflect the heart of service that Jesus modeled during His time on earth. Just as He washed the feet of His disciples, healed the sick, and fed the hungry, law enforcement officers meet the needs of their communities in countless ways, often without recognition or reward. But Galatians 6:9 reminds us that these efforts are not in vain. When we persevere in doing good, we are sowing seeds that will one day reap a harvest of blessings—both in this life and in eternity.

Perseverance is not about perfection; it's about persistence. It's about showing up, giving your best, and trusting God to use your efforts for His glory. For officers, this might mean handling a difficult case with patience, speaking kindly to someone in distress, or simply holding on to hope when the day feels heavy. In these moments, it's important to remember that perseverance doesn't mean doing it alone. God is with you, strengthening you, guiding you, and equipping you for the task at hand. Isaiah 40:31 says, "But they that wait upon the Lord shall renew their strength; they shall mount up with wings as eagles; they shall run, and not be weary; and they shall walk, and not faint." This promise reminds us that perseverance is not about relying on our own strength but about leaning on God's unfailing power.

The journey of perseverance is rarely easy, and it often feels lonely. Law enforcement officers, in particular, face unique challenges that can test their resolve and their faith. The long hours, the difficult decisions, and the emotional toll of the job can lead to exhaustion and discouragement. But Galatians 6:9 calls us to look beyond the weariness and focus on the reward. The harvest may not always be immediate, but it is certain. Every act of kindness, every moment of courage, and every decision to serve contributes to a greater purpose. For officers, this means knowing that their work matters—not just to the people they serve but to God Himself. He sees every sacrifice, every effort, and every moment of perseverance, and He promises to bring forth a harvest in due time.

As Christians, we are called to persevere in our own daily lives, whether it's through acts of service, moments of kindness, or simply staying faithful to God's calling. Perseverance is about trusting that even the smallest actions can have a ripple effect, touching lives in ways we may never fully understand. For law enforcement officers, this means recognizing that their work goes beyond enforcing laws—it's about building trust, fostering peace, and being a light in the darkness. It's about showing up for their communities, even when the challenges feel overwhelming, and trusting that God is working through them.

In moments of doubt or fatigue, it's helpful to reflect on the example of Jesus, who persevered through the ultimate challenges. He faced rejection, betrayal, and unimaginable suffering, yet He never wavered in His mission to save the world. His perseverance was rooted in love—a love so deep and unwavering that He gave His life for us. As followers of Christ, we are called to emulate His example, to serve others with the same selfless love, and to endure hardships with faith and hope. For law enforcement officers, this means finding strength in the knowledge that their perseverance reflects the character of Christ and serves as a testimony to His love.

Perseverance also requires community. Just as Jesus surrounded Himself with disciples, we are not meant to endure alone. For officers, this might mean leaning on their families, colleagues, or faith communities for support. It might mean finding strength in shared experiences, seeking encouragement from those who understand the challenges, and praying together for guidance and renewal. Galatians 6:2 reminds us, "Bear ye one another's burdens, and so fulfil the law of Christ." Perseverance is not about going it alone—it's about walking together in faith and trusting God to carry us through.

Ultimately, perseverance is about faithfulness—faithfulness to the calling God has placed on our lives, faithfulness to the people we serve, and faithfulness to the work He has entrusted to us. For law enforcement officers, this means continuing to show up, even when the road is tough, and trusting that their efforts are making a difference. It means remembering that God is with them in every moment, providing strength when they feel weak and encouragement when they feel weary. It means holding on to the promise of Galatians 6:9, knowing that in due season, their perseverance will bear fruit.

As we persevere in our own lives, let us remember that our efforts are part of a greater story—God's story of redemption and love. Whether we are serving in law enforcement, caring for our families, or simply striving to live out our faith, perseverance is a reflection of our trust in God's plan. It's about holding on to hope, even in the face of challenges, and trusting that our work is not in vain. Galatians 6:9 calls us to press on, knowing that our perseverance will one day be rewarded. Let us take heart in this promise and continue to serve with faith, courage, and love, trusting that God is with us every step of the way.

Day 3 - Patience Under Pressure

Patience under pressure is one of the greatest challenges and virtues in life, especially for those who carry the responsibility of protecting and serving others. For law enforcement officers, the ability to remain calm in the face of chaos, measured in moments of crisis, and composed during conflict is not just a skill—it is a necessity. Scripture underscores the value of such patience in Proverbs 16:32: "He that is slow to anger is better than the mighty: and he that ruleth his spirit than he that taketh a city." These words remind us that true strength is not found in brute force or quick reactions but in the quiet resilience of self-control, even under immense pressure. Officers often face situations that test their limits—escalating disputes, dangerous confrontations, or emotionally charged encounters—and the ability to respond with calm determination can mean the difference between resolution and escalation. This kind of patience is not simply about restraint; it is about choosing wisdom over impulse, grace over frustration, and peace over chaos. It reflects the heart of God, who is "slow to anger, and plenteous in mercy" (Psalm 103:8). To exercise patience under pressure is to embody a Christlike spirit, one that values understanding and compassion over reactionary decisions.

For an officer, the pressure can come in many forms—a high-stakes emergency, a heated exchange, or the relentless demands of the job. Each moment presents an opportunity to demonstrate a steady hand and a clear mind. Patience under pressure means pausing before responding, seeking wisdom in the chaos, and leaning on the strength that God provides. It is not a sign of weakness but of incredible strength, the kind that allows officers to defuse tension, maintain order, and protect those in their care. However, the challenges of remaining patient under pressure are not easily overcome. Human emotions naturally respond to stress with frustration, fear, or even anger, and it takes intentional effort to rule over these instincts. Proverbs 16:32 reminds us that the ability to control one's emotions is greater than physical might; it is an inner strength that comes from reliance on God's guidance and peace.

Jesus Himself modeled perfect patience under pressure throughout His ministry. When He was confronted by angry crowds, tested by His critics, or even betrayed by those closest to Him, He responded not with anger or haste but with wisdom and calm. In one particularly powerful moment, when the Pharisees brought a woman caught in adultery before Him, expecting Him to condemn her, Jesus knelt and wrote in the dust. Instead of rushing to judge, He responded with quiet authority, saying, "He that is without sin among you, let him first cast a stone at her" (John 8:7). His patience defused the situation, disarmed the accusers, and showed mercy to the woman. This example teaches us that patience allows for clarity, understanding, and grace, even in moments of immense pressure. Officers who strive to emulate this kind of patience serve not only as enforcers of the law but also as agents of peace and compassion in their communities.

Patience under pressure also requires a deep trust in God's sovereignty. In the heat of the moment, when decisions must be made quickly, there is comfort in knowing that God is in control, providing wisdom and guidance to those who seek Him. James 1:5 encourages us, "If any of you lack wisdom, let him ask of God, that giveth to all men liberally, and upbraideth not; and it shall be given him." This promise is a reminder that we are never alone in our struggles. Whether dealing with a stressful situation on the job or navigating the pressures of daily life, we can call on God for the strength to remain calm and patient. For officers, this might mean pausing for a brief prayer during a tense moment, seeking God's guidance before responding, or reflecting on His Word to stay grounded amidst chaos.

The ability to remain patient under pressure also has a profound impact on those around us. A calm presence can bring stability to a volatile situation, reassure those who are afraid, and demonstrate a commitment to fairness and justice. For officers, this influence extends not only to the people they serve but also to their colleagues and communities. When others see an officer exercising patience and self-control, they are more likely to respond in kind, creating a ripple effect of calm and cooperation. Proverbs 15:1 reminds us, "A soft answer turneth away wrath: but grievous words stir up anger." Patience, even in the most stressful circumstances, has the power to transform conflict into resolution and to replace fear with trust.

However, maintaining patience under pressure is not without its challenges. The physical and emotional toll of high-pressure situations can leave officers feeling drained, frustrated, or overwhelmed. In these moments, it is crucial to turn to God for renewal and strength. Isaiah 40:31 offers this encouragement: "But they that wait upon the Lord shall renew their strength; they shall mount up with wings as eagles; they shall run, and not be weary; and they shall walk, and not faint." Patience is not something we muster up on our own; it is a fruit of the Spirit, cultivated through prayer, faith, and reliance on God's grace. As Galatians 5:22-23 reminds us, "But the fruit of the Spirit is love, joy, peace, longsuffering, gentleness, goodness, faith, meekness, temperance." Longsuffering, or patience, is a divine attribute that reflects God's character in us.

For law enforcement officers, cultivating patience under pressure requires intentional practices. It might mean taking time to decompress after a difficult shift, seeking counsel from trusted mentors, or engaging in regular prayer and Scripture reading to stay spiritually grounded. It also means extending grace to oneself, recognizing that no one is perfect and that patience is a journey, not a destination. Just as officers are called to show understanding and compassion to others, they must also allow themselves room to grow and learn. Each moment of pressure is an opportunity to lean into God's strength, to practice patience, and to trust that He is working through them for His purposes.

Ultimately, patience under pressure is not just about staying calm—it is about reflecting the peace of Christ in every situation. It is about choosing to respond with wisdom instead of reacting in haste, seeking understanding instead of rushing to judgment, and trusting in God's timing instead of forcing our own solutions. For officers, this means being a steady presence in moments of uncertainty, a voice of reason in times of conflict, and a source of reassurance to those who are afraid. It means demonstrating that true strength is found not in power or control but in the quiet confidence of a heart anchored in God's peace.

As Proverbs 16:32 teaches, patience is greater than might, and self-control is more powerful than conquering a city. For those in law enforcement, this truth serves as both a challenge and an encouragement. It reminds us that patience is not a sign of weakness but a mark of true strength, a reflection of God's character, and a powerful tool for bringing peace to a world in need. Whether navigating the pressures of the job or facing challenges in daily life, may we all strive to embody the patience of Christ, trusting in His wisdom, leaning on His strength, and reflecting His peace in everything we do.

Day 4 - Prepared for Every Situation

Being prepared for every situation is a fundamental requirement for law enforcement officers, who daily face the unknown with courage, precision, and responsibility. They don their uniforms knowing that every call, every encounter, and every moment of their shift may bring challenges they cannot predict. It could be a life-threatening emergency, a moment of community connection, or a split-second decision with lasting consequences. This readiness requires more than physical training or mental alertness—it demands a steadfast heart and a clear mind, traits that mirror the spiritual vigilance God calls each of us to in 1 Peter 5:8: "Be sober, be vigilant; because your adversary the devil, as a roaring lion, walketh about, seeking whom he may devour." This verse is a clarion call for Christians to remain prepared in every aspect of life, to stand guard against spiritual threats with the same diligence that officers display when protecting their communities. The parallels between an officer's readiness and our spiritual vigilance are striking; just as officers equip themselves with tools, training, and strategy to respond effectively to danger, we are called to equip ourselves with faith, wisdom, and the Word of God to navigate life's uncertainties and stand firm against spiritual adversaries.

Officers prepare for their work by understanding the risks they may face and arming themselves with the tools to respond. Whether it's protective gear, communication devices, or knowledge of de-escalation tactics, their preparation reflects an understanding of the unpredictable nature of their calling. Similarly, Christians are called to prepare spiritually, equipping themselves with the "whole armor of God" to stand against the wiles of the enemy (Ephesians 6:11). This preparation begins with a sober mind—one that is clear, focused, and disciplined, not clouded by distractions or complacency. It continues with vigilance, a watchfulness that recognizes the spiritual battle at hand and remains ready to respond in faith, prayer, and action. To be spiritually vigilant is to live with a sense of awareness and purpose, knowing that while life may be filled with blessings, it is also marked by trials and challenges that require us to rely on God's strength and guidance.

The unpredictability of life mirrors the unpredictable situations officers face daily. No shift is ever the same, and no two calls are identical. This requires officers to approach each situation with humility, readiness, and an openness to adapt as needed. Spiritually, this same mindset applies; we cannot always anticipate the trials we will face, but we can prepare our hearts and minds to trust God and lean on His wisdom in every circumstance. Proverbs 3:5-6 reminds us, "Trust in the Lord with all thine heart; and lean not unto thine own understanding. In all thy ways acknowledge him, and he shall direct thy paths." This level of trust comes from consistent preparation—spending time in God's Word, building a life of prayer, and surrounding ourselves with a community of believers who encourage and strengthen our faith.

Just as officers train to respond to emergencies, Christians must also train their spiritual reflexes to respond to challenges with faith, love, and wisdom. This training involves immersing ourselves in Scripture so that when difficulties arise, we can draw from the truth of God's promises. It means developing a habit of prayer, not just in moments of crisis but as a daily practice that keeps us connected to God's will. It involves cultivating a spirit of discernment, allowing the Holy Spirit to guide our decisions and actions. Preparation is not about eliminating the unknown—it's about being ready to face it with confidence, knowing that God is with us and equips us for every challenge.

Officers know that preparation is not a one-time event; it is a continuous process. They review protocols, practice scenarios, and reflect on past experiences to improve their readiness. In the same way, spiritual vigilance requires ongoing effort. It means examining our hearts regularly, confessing our sins, and seeking God's grace to grow in holiness. It means staying alert to the subtle ways the enemy seeks to discourage, deceive, or distract us from our purpose. As 1 Peter 5:8 warns, the enemy prowls like a roaring lion, looking for opportunities to attack. But we are not called to face these attacks with fear; we are called to stand firm in the power of Christ, who has already won the ultimate victory over sin and death. When we prepare spiritually, we are not only defending ourselves but also positioning ourselves to be used by God to bring hope, peace, and truth to a world in need.

Preparation also involves trusting God with the outcomes. Officers may train extensively, but they cannot control every variable in a high-pressure situation. Similarly, Christians may prepare their hearts and minds, but they must ultimately trust that God's plan is greater than their understanding. Isaiah 41:10 offers this reassurance: "Fear thou not; for I am with thee: be not dismayed; for I am thy God: I will strengthen thee; yea, I will help thee; yea, I will uphold thee with the right hand of my righteousness." This promise reminds us that our preparation is not about relying solely on our strength but about partnering with God, who sustains and empowers us in every situation.

The value of preparation extends beyond individual readiness; it impacts those around us. When officers are prepared, their actions inspire trust and confidence in the communities they serve. In the same way, when Christians live with spiritual vigilance, their faith becomes a testimony to others. A prepared heart is one that can offer encouragement to the weary, wisdom to the confused, and hope to the brokenhearted. It is a heart that reflects the light of Christ, shining brightly even in the darkest moments. Matthew 5:16 reminds us, "Let your light so shine before men, that they may see your good works, and glorify your Father which is in heaven." This light is the result of a life prepared to glorify God in every circumstance, whether in times of joy or trial.

Being prepared for every situation also means being ready to respond to God's call at a moment's notice. Just as officers must be ready to act when duty calls, we must be ready to say yes to God's invitations, whether they come in the form of serving others, sharing the gospel, or stepping out in faith to fulfill His purpose for our lives. This readiness requires a willingness to let go of our plans and trust in His. It is a posture of surrender, rooted in the knowledge that God's ways are higher than ours (Isaiah 55:9) and that His timing is always perfect.

Ultimately, preparation is an act of faith. It is a recognition that while we cannot control every aspect of life, we can trust in the One who holds all things together. For law enforcement officers, this means approaching each shift with the assurance that their training and preparation will serve them well, while also leaning on God's guidance and protection. For Christians, it means living each day with a spirit of vigilance, ready to face whatever comes with courage and trust in God's promises. Whether the challenges we face are physical, emotional, or spiritual, we can find strength in the knowledge that God equips us for every situation and walks with us through it all.

In both the physical and spiritual realms, being prepared for every situation is not about eliminating uncertainty—it is about finding peace and purpose in the midst of it. It is about standing firm in faith, remaining vigilant against the enemy's schemes, and trusting that God's grace is sufficient for every challenge. As 1 Peter 5:8 calls us to be sober and vigilant, let us embrace this calling with steadfast hearts, ready to face each moment with the confidence that comes from knowing we are equipped by God, empowered by His Spirit, and held securely in His hands.

Day 5 - Power of Authority

The power of authority is a responsibility that carries both great privilege and profound accountability. For law enforcement officers, this authority is not just a badge or a title—it is a calling to uphold justice, protect the vulnerable, and serve with integrity. Every decision, every action, and every command carries weight, influencing lives and shaping communities. But amid this earthly authority, Romans 13:1 reminds us of a greater truth: "For there is no power but of God: the powers that be are ordained of God." This verse calls officers to see their authority as a gift and a responsibility that ultimately comes from God, the source of all power and justice. It is a humbling reminder that while officers are entrusted with significant earthly power, they are also stewards of a divine mission to reflect God's justice, mercy, and righteousness in their work. Every time an officer steps into their role, they are not only serving their community but also answering a higher call to honor the One who ordained their authority.

To wield authority well is to understand its purpose. Authority is not about dominance or control; it is about serving others, maintaining order, and ensuring peace. In this way, officers mirror the heart of God, who exercises His authority with both justice and compassion. Throughout Scripture, we see examples of God's perfect balance of power and mercy. He is a righteous judge who stands against evil, but He is also a loving Father who seeks restoration and redemption. For officers, this duality is reflected in their daily work as they enforce the law while showing care and understanding to those they encounter. It requires strength tempered by humility, courage guided by wisdom, and a deep awareness that their authority is not their own but entrusted to them by God.

The power of authority is not without its challenges. Officers often face situations where their decisions are scrutinized, their motives questioned, and their actions misunderstood. They must navigate the tension between upholding the law and extending grace, balancing firmness with fairness. In these moments, the knowledge that their authority comes from God provides both clarity and comfort. It reminds them that they are not acting on their own but are part of a larger purpose, one that reflects God's desire for justice and peace in the world. Romans 13:4 reinforces this truth, describing those in authority as "ministers of God to thee for good." This perspective shifts the focus from personal power to divine service, emphasizing that authority is not about self-interest but about fulfilling God's will for the good of others.

To exercise authority rightly, officers must first submit to the ultimate authority of God. This requires humility, a willingness to seek His guidance, and a commitment to align their actions with His principles. Micah 6:8 captures this beautifully: "He hath shewed thee, O man, what is good; and what doth the Lord require of thee, but to do justly, and to love mercy, and to walk humbly with thy God?" These words remind officers that their authority is not about elevating themselves but about walking in obedience to God's calling. It is about using their position to protect the innocent, stand against injustice, and promote peace, always keeping in mind that they are accountable to the One who gave them their power.

Authority also comes with the responsibility to reflect God's character. Jesus Himself demonstrated this perfectly during His time on earth. Though He had all authority in heaven and on earth (Matthew 28:18), He used His power to serve, heal, and teach. He washed His disciples' feet, fed the hungry, and defended the weak, showing that true authority is marked by selflessness and compassion. For officers, this example serves as a guide for how to lead with integrity and humility. It challenges them to use their authority not to assert dominance but to uplift others, protect the vulnerable, and create an environment where justice and mercy can thrive.

The weight of authority can be heavy, and officers may sometimes feel overwhelmed by the expectations placed upon them. In these moments, it is important to remember that God does not call anyone to a task without also equipping them for it. Philippians 4:13 offers this assurance: "I can do all things through Christ which strengtheneth me." This promise reminds officers that they do not bear the burden of authority alone. God provides the wisdom, strength, and courage needed to navigate the complexities of their role. By leaning on Him, officers can find the resilience to persevere, the clarity to make difficult decisions, and the peace to carry out their duties with confidence.

The power of authority also has the potential to influence others in profound ways. Officers who lead with integrity, fairness, and compassion set an example for their communities, inspiring trust and respect. Their actions can create a ripple effect, encouraging others to act justly and treat one another with kindness. This influence extends beyond the immediate impact of their work, leaving a lasting legacy of faithfulness and service. Matthew 5:16 speaks to this impact: "Let your light so shine before men, that they may see your good works, and glorify your Father which is in heaven." When officers exercise their authority in a way that reflects God's character, they become a light in their communities, pointing others to the ultimate source of justice and peace.

However, the responsibility of authority also requires vigilance. Romans 13:1 reminds us that all authority comes from God, which means it must be used in alignment with His will. This requires officers to continually examine their hearts, ensuring that their actions are motivated by justice, mercy, and love rather than pride or self-interest. It also means being open to correction, learning from mistakes, and seeking wisdom from God and others. Proverbs 3:5-6 offers this guidance: "Trust in the Lord with all thine heart; and lean not unto thine own understanding. In all thy ways acknowledge him, and he shall direct thy paths." By staying rooted in God's truth, officers can navigate the challenges of their authority with integrity and grace.

The power of authority is both a gift and a responsibility, one that requires constant dependence on God. For officers, this means approaching their work with humility, recognizing that their authority is not about their own power but about serving others and fulfilling God's purposes. It means seeking His guidance in every decision, trusting in His strength during difficult moments, and reflecting His love and justice in every interaction. It is a high calling, but it is also a deeply rewarding one, as it provides an opportunity to make a tangible difference in the lives of others.

Ultimately, the power of authority points back to the sovereignty of God. As Romans 13:1 reminds us, all power comes from Him, and those who exercise authority do so under His direction. This truth offers both comfort and accountability, reassuring officers that their work is part of God's greater plan while also challenging them to steward their authority wisely. Whether enforcing the law, resolving conflicts, or protecting the vulnerable, officers have the opportunity to reflect God's character and advance His kingdom on earth. It is a responsibility that requires strength, courage, and faith, but it is also a profound privilege—to serve as a minister of God's justice and peace, bringing hope and restoration to a broken world.

Day 6 - Pride in Service

Pride in service is not about arrogance or self-importance—it's about finding joy, purpose, and fulfillment in the work we are called to do, knowing that it makes a difference in the lives of others and honors God. For law enforcement officers, every shift begins with the understanding that their work matters deeply. Whether responding to emergencies, comforting those in crisis, or simply maintaining peace in their communities, officers serve with a sense of responsibility and commitment that reflects the heart of their calling. In Matthew 25:21, Jesus speaks these powerful words: "His lord said unto him, Well done, *thou* good and faithful servant: thou hast been faithful over a few things, I will make thee ruler over many things: enter thou into the joy of thy lord." This verse captures the essence of pride in service, reminding us that the ultimate reward for our efforts is the approval of our heavenly Father. Just as officers take pride in serving their communities with courage and integrity, we are all called to take pride in serving God and others, finding meaning and purpose in our acts of faithfulness, no matter how big or small.

True pride in service comes from knowing that the work we do is part of something greater than ourselves. For officers, this means recognizing that their role is not just about enforcing laws but about being a source of hope, stability, and compassion in a world that often feels chaotic and broken. It means understanding that every act of service—whether it's helping a child find their way home, de-escalating a dangerous situation, or simply showing kindness to someone in need—reflects God's love and justice. This kind of pride is not self-centered; it is rooted in gratitude for the opportunity to make a difference and in the desire to honor God through our actions. When we serve with this mindset, we reflect the heart of Jesus, who came not to be served but to serve and to give His life as a ransom for many (Mark 10:45).

For law enforcement officers, pride in service is often shaped by the challenges they face. The long hours, the difficult decisions, and the emotional toll of the job can be overwhelming, but they also create opportunities to demonstrate resilience, compassion, and faithfulness. Each shift is a chance to show up, give their best, and make a positive impact, even in the smallest ways. This commitment to excellence reflects the parable of the talents in Matthew

25, where the master commends his faithful servants for using what they were given to achieve great things. Like the servants in the parable, officers are entrusted with unique responsibilities and are called to use their skills, training, and resources to serve others with diligence and care. The pride they feel in their work is a testament to their dedication and a reminder that their efforts are seen and valued by God.

At the heart of pride in service is the recognition that every act of faithfulness, no matter how unnoticed or unappreciated it may seem, carries eternal significance. Jesus's words in Matthew 25:21 remind us that our service is not about seeking recognition from others but about honoring God with our lives. For officers, this means finding fulfillment not in accolades or praise but in the knowledge that their work is part of God's greater plan to bring justice, peace, and restoration to the world. It means trusting that even the smallest acts of kindness and courage can have a ripple effect, touching lives in ways they may never fully understand. Whether it's a word of encouragement to a colleague, a gesture of compassion to someone in need, or a moment of bravery in the face of danger, each act of service reflects the character of Christ and contributes to His kingdom.

Pride in service also involves a deep sense of gratitude for the opportunity to serve. For law enforcement officers, this gratitude may come from the privilege of making a difference in their communities, the camaraderie of working alongside dedicated colleagues, or the satisfaction of knowing they are fulfilling their calling. This gratitude fuels their commitment to excellence and motivates them to persevere, even in the face of adversity. In the same way, we are called to approach our service to God and others with a spirit of thankfulness, recognizing that every opportunity to serve is a gift from Him. Colossians 3:23 encourages us, "And whatsoever ye do, do *it* heartily, as to the Lord, and not unto men;" This verse reminds us that our service is ultimately an act of worship, a way of expressing our love and devotion to God.

However, pride in service must always be balanced with humility. While it is right to take joy and satisfaction in our work, we must also remember that our abilities, opportunities, and successes come from God. Philippians 2:3-4 challenges us, "Let nothing be done through strife or vainglory; but in lowliness of mind let each esteem other better than themselves. Look not every man on his own things, but every man also on the things of others." For officers, this means approaching their work with a servant's heart, putting the needs of others above their own and seeking to honor God in all they do. It means recognizing that their authority and influence are not for personal gain but for the good of others and the glory of God.

Pride in service is not just about what we do; it is about who we are becoming in the process. For law enforcement officers, their work shapes their character, teaching them perseverance, empathy, and courage. In the same way, our service to God and others helps us grow in our faith, develop Christlike qualities, and deepen our relationship with Him. As we serve, we are reminded of our dependence on God and our need for His guidance, strength, and grace. This dependence keeps us humble, focused, and grounded, allowing us to serve with integrity and joy.

Ultimately, pride in service is about living out our calling with faithfulness and love. It is about using our gifts, talents, and opportunities to make a difference in the lives of others and to glorify God. For officers, this means approaching each day with a sense of purpose and dedication, knowing that their work matters and that they are part of something greater than themselves. For all of us, it means serving with the same attitude, finding joy in the privilege of being part of God's plan and trusting that our efforts will bear fruit in His perfect timing. As Jesus said in Matthew 25:21, "Well done, thou good and faithful servant." These words are the ultimate affirmation, reminding us that our service, when done with faithfulness and love, is seen, valued, and celebrated by God. Let us take pride in our service, knowing that it is an expression of our love for Him and a reflection of His love for the world.

Day 7 - Protecting Boundaries

Protecting boundaries is essential for both maintaining order in a community and guarding the integrity of our hearts and minds. Law enforcement officers understand the importance of boundaries better than most; they are tasked with enforcing the lines that keep society safe, ensuring that chaos does not overrun peace, and intervening when boundaries are crossed to restore order. Their work is a constant reminder of the value of limits and discipline, both for individuals and communities. Similarly, in our spiritual lives, boundaries are vital. Psalm 141:3 says, "Set a watch, O LORD, before my mouth; keep the door of my lips." This verse highlights the necessity of protecting not just physical spaces but also the words we speak and the thoughts we allow to take root. Just as officers set clear lines to uphold laws and protect others, we are called to set spiritual boundaries that safeguard our hearts, minds, and relationships, ensuring that we remain aligned with God's will and resistant to the temptations and distractions of the world.

Boundaries are not restrictive; they are protective. For officers, boundaries define where danger begins and safety ends, helping them navigate their duties with precision and clarity. They ensure that people are held accountable while also protecting the innocent. In our spiritual lives, boundaries function in much the same way. They create a framework for us to live in obedience to God, shielding us from harmful influences and guiding us toward what is good and right. These boundaries are not about limiting our freedom but about ensuring that we walk in the freedom God intends for us—freedom from sin, guilt, and the burdens of a chaotic, undisciplined life. By setting a watch over our words, thoughts, and actions, as Psalm 141:3 encourages, we create a space where God's peace and presence can dwell.

The need for boundaries is rooted in the reality that we live in a world full of temptations, distractions, and influences that can pull us away from God's purpose. Just as officers remain vigilant to prevent crime and maintain order, we must remain vigilant to protect our spiritual health. Proverbs 4:23 warns us, "Keep thy heart with all diligence; for out of it *are* the issues of life." This verse reminds us that our hearts are the wellspring of our thoughts, actions, and decisions, and that guarding them requires intentional effort. Setting spiritual boundaries means being mindful of what we allow into our lives—whether through the media we consume, the relationships we nurture, or the habits we form. It means recognizing the areas where we are most vulnerable and putting safeguards in place to protect ourselves from falling into sin or becoming distracted from God's calling.

For law enforcement officers, maintaining boundaries is a daily discipline. They must remain alert, focused, and ready to act when those boundaries are threatened. This requires not only physical readiness but also mental and emotional discipline. Similarly, setting spiritual boundaries requires ongoing vigilance and commitment. It means regularly evaluating our priorities, assessing the influences in our lives, and making choices that align with God's truth. It also means relying on the Holy Spirit to guide us, convict us, and strengthen us when our boundaries are tested. Just as officers trust their training and instincts to uphold the law, we must trust God's Word and His Spirit to help us protect our hearts and live in obedience to Him.

One of the most important aspects of protecting boundaries is understanding their purpose. Boundaries are not about control or rigidity; they are about creating an environment where growth, healing, and flourishing can occur. For officers, boundaries ensure that communities can thrive in safety and order. For Christians, spiritual boundaries create the space for us to grow in our relationship with God, deepen our faith, and live out His purpose for our lives. They help us say no to the things that harm us so that we can say yes to the things that bring us closer to Him. This might mean setting limits on how we spend our time, choosing to walk away from toxic relationships, or guarding our words to ensure that they reflect God's love and truth. Psalm 141:3 reminds us that even our speech requires boundaries, as our words have the power to build up or tear down, to bring life or cause harm.

Protecting boundaries also requires humility and self-awareness. Just as officers must recognize their own limitations and seek support when needed, we must acknowledge our weaknesses and rely on God's strength to uphold our boundaries. This might mean seeking accountability from trusted friends or mentors, turning to Scripture for guidance, or spending time in prayer to ask for God's help. Philippians 4:13 reminds us, "I can do all things through Christ which strengtheneth me." This verse encourages us to trust that God will equip us to protect the boundaries He has called us to set, even when it feels difficult or overwhelming.

The practice of protecting boundaries is not just about defense; it is also about offense. By setting boundaries, we create space for what matters most—for worship, for service, for relationships that honor God, and for the pursuit of His will. Boundaries allow us to focus on what is truly important, free from the distractions and entanglements that can pull us away from our purpose. For officers, boundaries ensure that their work is effective and that they can fulfill their duty to protect and serve. For Christians, boundaries enable us to live lives that are focused, intentional, and aligned with God's mission.

However, protecting boundaries is not always easy. There will be times when they are tested, when the pressures of life or the influence of others tempt us to compromise or let our guard down. In these moments, it is crucial to remember that our boundaries are not just our own; they are rooted in God's truth and upheld by His power. Ephesians 6:10-11 reminds us, "Finally, my brethren, be strong in the Lord, and in the power of his might. Put on the whole armour of God, that ye may be able to stand against the wiles of the devil." This passage calls us to rely on God's strength and protection as we guard the boundaries He has given us, trusting that He will provide the wisdom and courage we need to stand firm.

Ultimately, protecting boundaries is an act of love—love for God, love for ourselves, and love for others. It is a way of honoring the life God has given us and stewarding it well. For law enforcement officers, setting boundaries is an expression of their commitment to the safety and well-being of their communities. For Christians, it is an expression of our commitment to living in obedience to God and reflecting His character in all that we do. It is a way of saying yes to His calling and no to anything that would hinder us from fulfilling it.

As we seek to protect boundaries in our lives, let us remember the words of Psalm 141:3 "Set a watch, O LORD, before my mouth; keep the door of my lips." This verse reminds us that God is our ultimate protector, the One who guards our hearts and guides our steps. When we entrust our boundaries to Him, we can live with confidence, knowing that He will strengthen us, sustain us, and lead us in the path of righteousness. Whether we are enforcing boundaries in our communities or guarding the boundaries of our hearts, may we do so with faith, courage, and a deep trust in the One who calls us to this important work.

Day 8 - Pursuing Truth

Pursuing truth is a lifelong mission, both in the field of law enforcement and in our spiritual lives. For officers, every investigation, every report, and every call to action is a search for the truth—a quest to uncover what has happened, to ensure justice is served, and to bring clarity to confusion. This pursuit requires determination, wisdom, and an unwavering commitment to fairness and integrity, knowing that truth is the foundation upon which justice and trust are built. In the same way, our spiritual journey is centered on seeking the ultimate truth found in God. Jesus declared in John 8:32, "And ye shall know the truth, and the truth shall make you free." This promise is profound, reminding us that truth is not just a set of facts or rules but a revelation that transforms us, sets us free from the chains of sin and deceit, and guides us into a life of purpose and peace. Just as officers diligently seek the truth to uphold justice in their communities, we are called to diligently pursue God's truth to guide our hearts, shape our decisions, and lead us closer to Him.

Truth is powerful, but it is also often elusive. In the world of law enforcement, uncovering the truth requires patience, discernment, and a willingness to look beyond surface appearances. Investigations often involve piecing together fragments of evidence, listening to conflicting accounts, and sifting through distractions and falsehoods to find the reality of what has occurred. Similarly, in our spiritual lives, the pursuit of truth requires us to dig deeper, to question the narratives the world offers us, and to seek God's perspective above all else. It requires us to go beyond the surface, to study His Word, to listen to His voice in prayer, and to discern His truth amid the noise and confusion of the world. Proverbs 3:5-6 reminds us, "Trust in the Lord with all thine heart; and lean not unto thine own understanding. In all thy ways acknowledge him, and he shall direct thy paths." This pursuit of God's truth is not always easy, but it is essential, as it forms the foundation of a life lived in freedom, purpose, and alignment with His will.

For law enforcement officers, pursuing truth is often fraught with challenges. There are times when the path to truth is obstructed by deceit, fear, or resistance, requiring them to persevere and remain committed to uncovering what is right. This mirrors the spiritual struggles we face when seeking God's truth in a world that often promotes falsehoods or half-truths. It takes courage to stand for what is right, especially when the truth challenges popular opinions or demands personal sacrifice. But Jesus's promise in John 8:32 reminds us that truth is worth pursuing, for it brings freedom—freedom from the lies that entangle us, from the fears that hold us back, and from the burdens of guilt and shame. The truth of God's love, grace, and purpose liberates us to live fully as He intended, anchored in the reality of who He is and who we are in Him.

Truth also has the power to restore and heal. In law enforcement, uncovering the truth can bring closure to victims, accountability to offenders, and peace to communities. It has the potential to mend what has been broken and to bring light into situations shrouded in darkness. In our spiritual lives, God's truth does the same. It reveals His love for us, His plan for our lives, and His promise of redemption. It reminds us that no matter how far we may have strayed, His truth is constant and unchanging, inviting us back into His embrace. Psalm 119:105 says, "NUN. Thy word *is* a lamp unto my feet, and a light unto my path." This verse illustrates how God's truth illuminates our way, guiding us through life's uncertainties and showing us the steps we need to take.

However, pursuing truth requires humility. For officers, this means setting aside personal biases, approaching each situation with an open mind, and allowing the facts to lead them to the truth rather than preconceived notions. In our spiritual lives, humility means acknowledging that we don't have all the answers and that God's wisdom far surpasses our understanding. Isaiah 55:8-9 reminds us, "For my thoughts are not your thoughts, neither are your ways my ways, saith the LORD. For as the heavens are higher than the earth, so are my ways higher than your ways, and my thoughts than your thoughts." This humility allows us to trust God's truth, even when it challenges our own perceptions or desires, and to surrender our will to His.

Pursuing truth also requires perseverance. Just as officers must remain steadfast in their investigations, often facing obstacles and setbacks, we must remain steadfast in our spiritual pursuit of God's truth. There will be times when the answers seem unclear, when doubts arise, or when the path forward feels uncertain. In these moments, we are called to cling to God's promises and to continue seeking Him with all our hearts. Jeremiah 29:13 assures us, "And ye shall seek me, and find *me*, when ye shall search for me with all your heart." This promise encourages us to remain committed to the pursuit of truth, trusting that God will reveal Himself to us as we seek Him earnestly.

The pursuit of truth also transforms us. As we seek God's truth, we are changed by it, becoming more like Him in character and purpose. Truth shapes our values, guides our decisions, and empowers us to live with integrity and courage. For law enforcement officers, the pursuit of truth is not just about resolving cases; it is about upholding justice, serving with honor, and building trust within their communities. For Christians, the pursuit of God's truth is not just about gaining knowledge; it is about living in alignment with His will, reflecting His love, and sharing His truth with others. Ephesians 4:15 encourages us to speak the truth in love, "But speaking the truth in love, may grow up into him in all things, which is the head, *even* Christ:" This verse reminds us that truth is not just something we seek but something we live and share, bringing light and hope to those around us.

Ultimately, pursuing truth is about seeking Jesus, who declared in John 14:6, "Jesus saith unto him, I am the way, the truth, and the life: no man cometh unto the Father, but by me." Jesus is the embodiment of truth, and in knowing Him, we find the ultimate freedom and fulfillment we long for. His truth sets us free from the lies of the enemy, the weight of sin, and the fear of the unknown. It gives us a firm foundation to stand on, a clear purpose to live for, and an unshakable hope for the future. Just as law enforcement officers dedicate themselves to uncovering the truth in their work, we are called to dedicate ourselves to knowing and living God's truth in every aspect of our lives.

As we pursue truth, let us do so with the same diligence, courage, and integrity that officers bring to their work. Let us approach God's Word with open hearts, seeking His guidance and wisdom. Let us remain steadfast in our pursuit, trusting that His truth will lead us into freedom and peace. And let us live out His truth in our words, actions, and relationships, becoming beacons of His love and light in a world that desperately needs it. For in knowing the truth, we are not only set free—we are also empowered to live fully for the One who is truth itself.

Day 9 - Peace Amidst Chaos

Peace amidst chaos is a gift that feels almost unimaginable in a world filled with noise, tension, and uncertainty. For law enforcement officers, chaos is not just a passing moment; it is often the backdrop of their daily work. Whether responding to emergencies, calming conflicts, or navigating unpredictable situations, officers step into the turmoil to bring order, safety, and resolution. Yet, in the midst of this outward chaos, the promise of inner peace becomes not only essential but life-sustaining. Jesus's words in John 14:27 are a powerful assurance: "Peace I leave with you, my peace I give unto you: not as the world giveth, give I unto you. Let not your heart be troubled, neither let it be afraid." This peace, unlike the fleeting calm the world offers, is unshakable and enduring—a peace that anchors the soul even when everything around it seems to fall apart. Just as officers must remain steady and focused in chaotic situations, we, too, are called to carry God's peace within us, trusting in His presence and promises to sustain us no matter the circumstances.

Chaos comes in many forms—external conflicts, internal struggles, and the unpredictable challenges that life throws our way. For officers, chaos might mean responding to a high-stakes situation, managing the emotions of those involved, or making critical decisions in moments of crisis. For the rest of us, chaos may manifest as overwhelming responsibilities, relational conflicts, or the fears and uncertainties that keep us up at night. In both cases, the pressure of chaos can feel suffocating, draining our energy and clouding our judgment. But Jesus's promise of peace is not contingent on the absence of chaos; it is a peace that exists within it, a calm that steadies us even when the storm rages around us. Philippians 4:7 states "And the peace of God, which passeth all understanding, shall keep your hearts and minds through Christ Jesus." a divine gift that guards our hearts and minds in Christ Jesus. This peace doesn't come from our circumstances; it comes from knowing that God is in control, that He is with us, and that His love is greater than any challenge we face.

For law enforcement officers, maintaining peace amidst chaos is both a professional necessity and a personal challenge. They are called to be the calm in the storm, to bring clarity and order to situations where emotions run high and dangers loom large. This requires not only training and experience but also an inner strength that allows them to remain composed and compassionate in the face of adversity. Similarly, as followers of Christ, we are called to embody His peace in a world that often feels chaotic and uncertain. This means trusting in His sovereignty, leaning on His strength, and allowing His Spirit to guide us through life's challenges. Isaiah 26:3 offers this reassurance: "Thou wilt keep him in perfect peace, whose mind is stayed on thee: because he trusteth in thee." By fixing our hearts and minds on God, we can experience a peace that transcends our circumstances, enabling us to stand firm and unshaken even in the most turbulent times.

The peace that Jesus gives is not passive; it is active and transformative. It is a peace that equips us to face chaos with courage, to respond to conflict with grace, and to bring hope to those who are hurting. For officers, this peace allows them to approach their work with clarity and purpose, knowing that they are not alone in their efforts. For all of us, it empowers us to navigate the challenges of life with confidence and faith, trusting that God's presence goes before us, behind us, and beside us. This peace is not the absence of struggle but the assurance that God is with us in the struggle, working all things together for our good (Romans 8:28). It is a reminder that no matter how chaotic life may feel, we are held securely in His hands.

Peace amidst chaos also requires intentionality. Just as officers must train and prepare to handle high-pressure situations, we must cultivate habits that anchor us in God's peace. This means spending time in prayer, immersing ourselves in His Word, and seeking His presence daily. Psalm 46:10 encourages us to "Be still, and know that I *am* God: I will be exalted among the heathen, I will be exalted in the earth." In the stillness, we find the reassurance that God is in control, that He is greater than the chaos around us, and that His peace is available to us at all times. This intentional pursuit of peace allows us to carry His calm into every situation, becoming a source of strength and hope for those around us.

However, maintaining peace amidst chaos is not always easy. There will be moments when the noise of life feels overwhelming, when fear and doubt threaten to consume us, and when the chaos seems too great to bear. In these moments, it is crucial to remember that God's peace is not something we have to manufacture on our own; it is a gift He freely gives to those who seek Him. Matthew 11:28-29 invites us to come to Jesus with our burdens and find rest in

Him: "Come unto me, all ye that labour and are heavy laden, and I will give you rest. Take my yoke upon you, and learn of me; for I am meek and lowly in heart: and ye shall find rest unto your souls." This rest, this peace, is a reminder that we do not have to carry the weight of chaos alone. God walks with us, strengthens us, and fills us with His peace even in the midst of life's storms.

The peace of God is not only for our benefit; it is also a gift we are called to share with others. Just as officers bring peace to their communities through their work, we are called to be peacemakers in our relationships, our workplaces, and our world. Matthew 5:9 says, "Blessed *are* the peacemakers: for they shall be called the children of God." As recipients of God's peace, we have the privilege and responsibility to extend that peace to those around us, becoming conduits of His love and grace in a world that desperately needs it. This might mean offering a listening ear to someone in distress, speaking words of encouragement to someone who feels overwhelmed, or simply being a calm and steady presence in the midst of chaos.

Ultimately, peace amidst chaos is not about avoiding the challenges of life but about facing them with the confidence that comes from knowing we are never alone. It is about trusting in the promises of God, leaning on His strength, and allowing His peace to guard our hearts and minds. For law enforcement officers, this peace is a source of resilience and clarity as they navigate the demands of their work. For all of us, it is a reminder that no matter what we face, we are held by a God who loves us, who is for us, and who is greater than any chaos we encounter. As we rest in His peace, we find the strength to persevere, the courage to stand firm, and the hope to keep moving forward. In a world that often feels overwhelming, may we carry His peace within us, allowing it to guide us, sustain us, and shine through us as a testimony to His unfailing love.

Day 10 - Partnering with Others

Partnering with others is a powerful and essential part of life, whether in the field of law enforcement, where teamwork is vital for safety and success, or in our spiritual journey, where collaboration and fellowship strengthen our faith and purpose. For officers, the importance of partnership cannot be overstated. From navigating dangerous situations to solving complex cases, they rely on their teammates for support, insight, and shared responsibility. This reliance fosters trust and unity, creating bonds that are often as strong as family. Ecclesiastes 4:9 captures this truth beautifully: "Two *are* better than one; because they have a good reward for their labour." This verse reminds us that together we can accomplish more, face challenges with greater resilience, and experience the joy of shared success. In the same way, our walk with the Lord is not meant to be walked alone. God calls us to partner with others in faith, building relationships that encourage, inspire, and challenge us to grow in Him.

The power of partnership lies in its ability to multiply strength, wisdom, and perseverance. Just as officers rely on one another to cover blind spots, share the load, and ensure each other's safety, we rely on our faith partners to encourage us, hold us accountable, and help us see God's perspective when our own vision is clouded. Life's challenges often feel overwhelming when faced alone, but with a partner—a friend, a mentor, a spouse, or a spiritual leader—we find strength we didn't know we had. Proverbs 27:17 says, "Iron sharpeneth iron; so a man sharpeneth the countenance of his friend." This imagery speaks to the refining and strengthening power of relationships, showing how God uses others to shape us into the people He created us to be.

For law enforcement officers, teamwork is a matter of life and death. In high-pressure situations, they must trust their partners implicitly, knowing that their lives and the lives of others may depend on that trust. This same principle applies to our spiritual partnerships. As we navigate the trials and uncertainties of life, we need people we can lean on, people who will point us back to God when we feel lost, and people who will stand beside us in prayer and encouragement. Galatians 6:2 reminds us, "Bear ye one another's burdens, and so fulfil the law of Christ." This act of bearing each other's burdens is at the heart of partnership, demonstrating the love and compassion that Christ calls us to share.

Partnerships also provide a sense of accountability that helps us stay grounded and focused. In the field, officers work together to ensure that each member of the team is upholding their responsibilities and acting with integrity. Similarly, in our spiritual lives, having partners in faith keeps us accountable to our commitments, our values, and our walk with God. These partnerships challenge us to grow, to step out in faith, and to remain steadfast in our purpose. Hebrews 10:24-25 encourages us, "And let us consider one another to provoke unto love and to good works: Not forsaking the assembling of ourselves together, as the manner of some is; but exhorting one another: and so much the more, as ye see the day approaching." Through fellowship and partnership, we inspire and strengthen one another to live out our faith boldly and faithfully.

Partnering with others also reminds us of our shared humanity and the beauty of diversity within the body of Christ. Just as officers bring different skills, perspectives, and experiences to their teams, we each bring unique gifts and talents to our spiritual partnerships. 1 Corinthians 12:12-14 describes this beautifully, comparing believers to the parts of a body, each with its own function but all working together for the good of the whole. When we partner with others, we benefit from their strengths, learn from their experiences, and see the world through their eyes. This collaboration enriches our lives and deepens our understanding of God's love and purpose.

However, building and maintaining partnerships requires effort, humility, and intentionality. For officers, this means setting aside ego, communicating openly, and working together toward a common goal. In our spiritual lives, it means being willing to invest time and energy into relationships, to forgive when conflicts arise, and to prioritize unity over personal preferences. Ephesians 4:2-3 encourages us, "With all lowliness and meekness, with longsuffering, forbearing one another in love; Endeavouring to keep the unity of the Spirit in the bond of peace." This commitment to unity reflects God's desire for His people to work together in harmony, supporting and uplifting one another as we pursue His mission.

Partnerships also remind us of our dependence on God. While teamwork strengthens us, our ultimate reliance is on Him, the One who unites and equips us for His purposes. Philippians 2:13 reassures us, "For it is God which worketh in you both to will and to do of *his* good pleasure." This divine partnership is the foundation of all our relationships, enabling us to love, serve, and support others as He has loved and supported us. When we partner with others in faith, we become co-laborers with Christ, working together to share His love and light with the world.

The rewards of partnership are profound. For officers, a strong team can mean the difference between success and failure, safety and danger. For believers, spiritual partnerships provide encouragement, wisdom, and a sense of belonging that strengthens our faith and empowers us to live out our calling. These relationships remind us that we are not alone, that we are part of a larger community united by a shared love for God and a desire to serve Him. Together, we can accomplish more than we ever could on our own, reflecting the truth of Ecclesiastes 4:9: "Two *are* better than one; because they have a good reward for their labour."

Ultimately, partnering with others is an act of love and obedience to God's design for community. It is a recognition that we are stronger together, that our differences are a gift, and that our shared faith unites us in a common purpose. Whether in the high-stakes world of law enforcement or the quiet moments of everyday life, partnerships remind us of the beauty and power of connection. They teach us to rely on one another, to celebrate each other's successes, and to support one another in times of need. Most importantly, they draw us closer to God, who is the ultimate partner in all we do.

As we seek to partner with others in faith, let us do so with humility, gratitude, and a commitment to love and unity. Let us embrace the opportunities God gives us to walk alongside others, to learn from them, and to share in their journeys. And let us remember that in partnering with others, we are fulfilling His command to love one another, building relationships that reflect His glory and advance His kingdom. Whether in moments of triumph or trial, may we find strength, joy, and purpose in the partnerships God has placed in our lives, knowing that together, we can accomplish far more than we ever could alone.

Day 11 - Perception and Discernment

Perception and discernment are vital in every aspect of life, and their importance becomes even clearer in high-stakes roles like law enforcement. Officers are tasked daily with making quick, accurate decisions based on incomplete information, relying on their training, instincts, and judgment to read situations accurately and respond wisely. However, even the best training cannot fully prepare them for the complexities and unpredictability of human behavior. This is where discernment comes into play—seeing beyond appearances, understanding deeper truths, and making decisions guided by wisdom rather than assumption. Similarly, in our spiritual lives, we are called to cultivate perception and discernment, seeking God's wisdom to navigate the complexities of life. 1 Samuel 16:7 reminds us, "But the LORD said unto Samuel, Look not on his countenance, or on the height of his stature; because I have refused him: for *the LORD seeth* not as man seeth; for man looketh on the outward appearance, but the LORD looketh on the heart." This verse underscores the need to go beyond surface-level judgments, inviting us to align our perspective with God's and to seek His guidance in every decision.

In the world of law enforcement, perception is often the difference between conflict and resolution, safety and danger, or justice and error. Officers must learn to read body language, interpret behavior, and assess risks with clarity and precision. But even the most experienced officers know that appearances can be deceiving. A calm exterior may hide inner turmoil, while someone who seems defensive may simply be frightened. Discernment allows officers to look deeper, to ask the right questions, and to respond with both wisdom and empathy. This mirrors the spiritual discernment we are called to develop as believers. Life often presents us with choices and challenges that are not as clear-cut as they seem. People may present one face while hiding another, and situations that appear promising may harbor unseen dangers. Without God's guidance, our limited perception can lead us astray. Proverbs 3:5-6 encourages us, "Trust in the LORD with all thine heart; and lean not unto thine own understanding. In all thy ways acknowledge him, and he shall direct thy paths." This reliance on God's wisdom is the foundation of true discernment, allowing us to see beyond what is visible and to act in alignment with His truth.

Discernment is not about suspicion or cynicism; it is about clarity and wisdom. It is the ability to see things as they truly are, to separate truth from falsehood, and to recognize the hand of God even in the midst of uncertainty. For officers, this means looking past stereotypes, biases, or assumptions and striving to understand the unique circumstances of each person or situation. It means being attuned to the subtle cues that reveal deeper truths and responding with fairness and compassion. In our spiritual lives, discernment means seeking God's perspective in all things—asking for His insight, listening for His voice, and aligning our decisions with His will. James 1:5 offers this promise: "If any of you lack wisdom, let him ask of God, that giveth to all *men* liberally, and upbraideth not; and it shall be given him." This assurance reminds us that God is eager to grant us the wisdom we need if we only ask.

One of the greatest challenges in developing discernment is overcoming our tendency to rely on appearances. As humans, we are naturally drawn to what we can see, hear, and touch, often allowing surface-level impressions to shape our opinions and decisions. Yet, Scripture repeatedly warns us against judging by outward appearances. In 1 Samuel 16:7, God reminds Samuel that His judgment is not based on what is visible but on the heart. This lesson is a call to humility, reminding us that our perspective is limited and that true understanding comes only from God. It challenges us to look beyond the surface, to seek the deeper truths that only God can reveal, and to trust in His ability to guide us when our own understanding falls short.

For law enforcement officers, this challenge is especially significant. Their work often requires them to make decisions under pressure, relying on split-second judgments that can have lasting consequences. In these moments, discernment becomes their greatest asset, allowing them to respond not just with logic but with wisdom and compassion. Similarly, in our spiritual lives, discernment equips us to navigate the complexities of relationships, responsibilities, and challenges with grace and integrity. It allows us to recognize God's presence in unexpected places, to see His purpose in difficult circumstances, and to trust His plan even when it is not immediately clear.

Developing discernment requires intentional effort and a deep connection to God. It begins with a commitment to seek His wisdom through prayer, Scripture, and reflection. Psalm 119:105 reminds us, "NUN. Thy word *is* a lamp unto my feet, and a light unto my path." God's Word illuminates our way, offering clarity and guidance in times of uncertainty. It also requires humility—a willingness to acknowledge our limitations and to surrender our understanding to God's greater wisdom. This humility opens the door for the Holy Spirit to work in us, shaping our perspective and helping us see with spiritual eyes.

Discernment also grows through experience. Just as officers learn to hone their perception through years of practice, we develop spiritual discernment through our walk with God. Each challenge, decision, and interaction becomes an opportunity to learn, to grow, and to deepen our reliance on Him. Romans 12:2 encourages us, "And be not conformed to this world: but be ye transformed by the renewing of your mind, that ye may prove what *is* that good, and acceptable, and perfect, will of God." This transformation allows us to discern God's will, aligning our thoughts and actions with His purpose and truth.

At its core, discernment is an act of love. It is the willingness to look beyond appearances, to seek the truth with humility, and to act with compassion and integrity. For officers, this means treating every person they encounter with dignity and respect, striving to understand their circumstances and responding in a way that reflects both justice and mercy. For believers, it means seeking God's wisdom in our relationships, decisions, and interactions, allowing His truth to shape our actions and attitudes. It means recognizing the image of God in every person we meet, even those who challenge or misunderstand us, and responding with grace and kindness.

Ultimately, discernment reflects God's character. Just as He sees us fully—our hearts, our struggles, and our potential—He calls us to see others through His eyes. This perspective transforms the way we approach every aspect of life, from our relationships to our responsibilities. It reminds us that true understanding comes not from our own abilities but from a deep connection to the One who knows all things. As we seek to develop discernment, let us remember the words of 1 Samuel 16:7: "But the LORD said unto Samuel, Look not on his countenance, or on the height of his stature; because I have refused him: for *the LORD seeth* not as man seeth; for man looketh on the outward appearance, but the LORD looketh on the heart." Let us strive to see as He sees, to act as He leads, and to live as a reflection of His truth and love.

Day 12 - Praising God in Success

Praising God in success is a humbling, joyful acknowledgment that all good things come from Him, and it is a vital part of living a life of gratitude and faith. For law enforcement officers, moments of success—whether resolving a complex case, saving a life, or seeing justice served—are times of relief and celebration. These victories are hard-earned, often the result of teamwork, perseverance, and courage, but even the most skilled officers know that success is never guaranteed. There are countless variables outside their control, and the outcome often depends on factors they cannot influence. This reality mirrors the broader truth for all of us: our successes, great and small, are ultimately gifts from God, reminders of His faithfulness, provision, and grace. 1 Thessalonians 5:18 states "In every thing give thanks: for this is the will of God in Christ Jesus concerning you." a command that challenges us to recognize God's hand not only in our triumphs but in every aspect of our lives. Just as officers celebrate victories while remaining mindful of the challenges they face, we are called to celebrate our successes with a heart of gratitude, always giving credit to the One who makes them possible.

Success, whether it comes in the form of personal achievements, professional milestones, or answered prayers, is a moment to pause and reflect on God's goodness. It is easy to take credit for our victories, attributing them to our efforts, talents, or determination, but Scripture reminds us that every good thing comes from God. James 1:17 declares, "Every good gift and every perfect gift is from above, and cometh down from the Father of lights, with whom is no variableness, neither shadow of turning." This truth shifts our perspective, helping us see that our abilities, opportunities, and outcomes are all part of God's provision. For law enforcement officers, this might mean recognizing God's guidance in a split-second decision, His protection during a dangerous situation, or His wisdom in resolving a conflict. For all of us, it means seeing His hand in the doors that open, the challenges we overcome, and the goals we achieve.

Praising God in success is an act of humility and faith. It requires us to acknowledge that we are not the source of our own success, that our victories are not solely the result of our hard work or intelligence, but the outcome of God's favor and faithfulness. This humility does not diminish our efforts; rather, it elevates our understanding of God's role in our lives, reminding us that He is the ultimate author of our story. Proverbs 3:5-6 encourages us, "Trust in the LORD with all thine heart; and lean not unto thine own understanding. In all thy ways acknowledge him, and he shall direct thy paths." When we acknowledge God in our successes, we align our hearts with His, recognizing that He is the source of all we have and all we accomplish.

Gratitude is the foundation of praise, and it transforms the way we experience success. Instead of seeing our achievements as endpoints, we see them as opportunities to glorify God and to bless others. Praising God in success keeps our focus on Him, preventing pride from taking root and reminding us that our purpose is not to exalt ourselves but to honor Him. This perspective is especially important for law enforcement officers, whose victories often involve the well-being of others. Celebrating these moments with gratitude to God reinforces their mission to serve with integrity and compassion, acknowledging that their success is part of a greater plan to bring justice, peace, and hope to their communities.

Success is also an opportunity to testify to God's goodness. When we give credit to Him for our victories, we share a powerful message of faith and dependence on His provision. Psalm 105:1 exhorts us, "O give thanks unto the LORD; call upon his name: make known his deeds among the people." By praising God openly, we not only deepen our own faith but also encourage others to see His work in their lives. For officers, this might mean sharing how prayer guided their decisions, how God's protection kept them safe, or how His wisdom brought clarity to a difficult situation. For all of us, it means using our successes as a platform to declare God's faithfulness, pointing others to the One who is worthy of all praise.

Praising God in success does not mean ignoring the challenges or struggles that precede it. Often, success comes after a season of hardship, uncertainty, or perseverance, making the victory all the more meaningful. Recognizing God's role in our success allows us to see how He was present in every step of the journey, providing strength when we were weak, guidance when we were lost, and hope when we were discouraged. This perspective deepens our gratitude and reminds us that our success is part of a larger story of His faithfulness. Romans 8:28 assures us, "And we know that all things work together for good to them that love God, to them who are the called according to *his* purpose." By praising Him in success, we affirm that His plans for us are good, even when the path to those plans is difficult.

Moreover, praising God in success prepares us for the next challenge. Success is not the end of the journey; it is a moment of rest and celebration before moving forward. For officers, each victory is followed by new calls, new cases, and new responsibilities. For believers, each answered prayer or accomplished goal is a stepping stone to the next chapter of God's plan for our lives. By praising Him in our successes, we renew our trust in His guidance and provision, equipping ourselves to face whatever comes next with confidence and faith. Philippians 4:6-7 encourages us, "Be careful for nothing; but in every thing by prayer and supplication with thanksgiving let your requests be made known unto God. And the peace of God, which passeth all understanding, shall keep your hearts and minds through Christ Jesus." This peace, born of gratitude and trust, sustains us as we continue to follow His lead.

Success is also an opportunity to bless others. Just as God's blessings flow into our lives, He calls us to share those blessings with others, using our success to serve, encourage, and uplift those around us. For officers, this might mean mentoring a colleague, supporting a community initiative, or simply being a source of hope and reassurance to those they serve. For all of us, it means using our time, talents, and resources to make a positive impact, reflecting God's love and generosity in our actions. 2 Corinthians 9:8 reminds us, "And God *is* able to make all grace abound toward you; that ye, always having all sufficiency in all *things*, may abound to every good work." By praising God in our successes and sharing His blessings, we become vessels of His grace, spreading His love and light to a world in need.

Ultimately, praising God in success is about keeping our hearts aligned with Him. It is about recognizing that every victory, no matter how small or great, is a gift from the One who loves us and works all things for our good. It is about cultivating a spirit of gratitude that transforms the way we see ourselves, our achievements, and our purpose. As we give thanks to God for our successes, we deepen our relationship with Him, strengthen our faith, and reflect His glory in all that we do. May we never forget that our successes are not ours alone—they are evidence of His faithfulness, His provision, and His unending love. Let us celebrate them with hearts full of gratitude, giving all praise and honor to the One who makes them possible.

Day 13 - Patrolling with Purpose

Patrolling with purpose is more than just a duty; it's a calling, a deliberate act of moving forward with intention, guided by a mission that brings meaning to every step. For law enforcement officers, patrolling is not just about covering ground or watching for disturbances; it's about serving their community, protecting those in need, and standing as a visible presence of safety and order. Every step they take is purposeful, driven by their commitment to uphold justice, ensure peace, and make a difference in the lives of others. Similarly, in our spiritual lives, we are called to walk with purpose, allowing each step to be guided by God's wisdom and aligned with His plan for us. Psalm 37:23 reminds us, "The steps of a *good* man are ordered by the LORD: and he delighteth in his way." This verse speaks to the beauty and assurance of living a life that follows God's direction—a life where every decision, every path, and every moment is infused with meaning because it is part of His divine design.

For officers, patrolling with purpose requires focus, awareness, and a deep understanding of their mission. They don't walk aimlessly or react without thought; instead, they observe, assess, and act with clarity and resolve. This mirrors the way we are called to live as believers, walking through life not as wanderers but as people with a clear sense of direction and purpose. God has given each of us a unique calling, and He promises to guide our steps as we trust in Him. Proverbs 3:5-6 reminds us, "Trust in the LORD with all thine heart; and lean not unto thine own understanding. In all thy ways acknowledge him, and he shall direct thy paths." This promise encourages us to rely on God's guidance, knowing that He is actively leading us toward His purpose, even when the way forward seems uncertain.

Purpose gives meaning to every step, even in the mundane or challenging moments. For officers, the act of patrolling might seem routine, but it is filled with opportunities to make a difference—to prevent harm, to build trust, and to be a source of reassurance to their community. In the same way, our daily walk with God is filled with moments that may seem ordinary but are deeply significant in His plan. Every interaction, every decision, and every step we take is an opportunity to reflect His love, share His truth, and fulfill His purpose for our lives. Colossians 3:23 encourages us, "And whatsoever ye do, do *it* heartily, as to the Lord, and not unto men;" This perspective transforms even the smallest tasks into acts of worship, reminding us that our purpose is not about seeking recognition from others but about honoring God with our lives.

Walking with purpose also requires trust and perseverance. Just as officers face challenges, uncertainties, and moments of danger in their patrols, we encounter obstacles and trials in our spiritual journey. There are times when the path ahead is unclear, when the weight of our responsibilities feels overwhelming, or when the distractions of life threaten to pull us off course. In these moments, it is crucial to remember that we are not walking alone. God is with us, guiding our steps, providing strength, and equipping us for the journey. Isaiah 41:10 offers this reassurance: "Fear thou not; for I *am* with thee: be not dismayed; for I *am* thy God: I will strengthen thee; yea, I will help thee; yea, I will uphold thee with the right hand of my righteousness." This promise reminds us that our purpose is not something we carry on our own; it is sustained by God's presence and power.

Patrolling with purpose also involves being present and attentive. Officers know that their work requires vigilance and a constant awareness of their surroundings. They must be ready to respond to the unexpected, to adapt to changing circumstances, and to make decisions that align with their mission. Similarly, walking with purpose as believers means being attuned to God's voice, sensitive to His leading, and open to the opportunities He places before us. It means living with intentionality, seeking His guidance in our choices, and being faithful to the tasks He has entrusted to us. Ephesians 5:15-16 encourages us, "See then that ye walk circumspectly, not as fools, but as wise, Redeeming the time, because the days are evil." This call to walk wisely and make the most of every opportunity reminds us that our purpose is not only about where we are going but also about how we live along the way.

Purpose also brings clarity to our priorities. For officers, their mission to serve and protect shapes the way they spend their time, energy, and resources. It helps them stay focused on what matters most, even when distractions or challenges arise. In our spiritual lives, our purpose in following God's will provides the same clarity. It reminds us to prioritize His kingdom above all else, to seek His righteousness, and to trust that He will provide for our needs. Matthew 6:33 captures this beautifully: "But seek ye first the kingdom of God, and his righteousness; and all these things shall be added unto you." By keeping our focus on God's purpose, we can navigate life's demands with a sense of peace and direction, knowing that He is in control.

Walking with purpose also means walking in faith. There are times when the path God calls us to take may not make sense from a human perspective, when the steps ahead seem uncertain or even impossible. In these moments, we are called to trust in His promises and to move forward in obedience, knowing that His plans are always good. Hebrews 11:1 reminds us, "Now faith is the substance of things hoped for, the evidence of things not seen." This faith allows us to walk with confidence, even when we cannot see the full picture, trusting that God is leading us toward His perfect plan.

Patrolling with purpose is not just about the destination; it is about the journey. For officers, every patrol is an opportunity to serve, to build relationships, and to make a positive impact. For believers, every step of our journey with God is an opportunity to grow in faith, to reflect His character, and to fulfill His purpose for our lives. It is a reminder that our purpose is not just about what we accomplish but about who we become as we walk with Him. As we follow His guidance, we are transformed by His love, strengthened by His grace, and equipped to live out His mission in the world.

Ultimately, patrolling with purpose is about living a life that honors God and aligns with His will. It is about recognizing that every step we take is part of a larger story, a story written by the One who knows us, loves us, and has a plan for our lives. Psalm 37:23 assures us, "The steps of a *good* man are ordered by the LORD: and he delighteth in his way." This promise reminds us that our purpose is not something we have to figure out on our own; it is something God reveals to us as we walk with Him in faith and obedience. As we patrolling with purpose, may we do so with hearts full of gratitude, trust, and joy, knowing that we are part of His greater plan and that every step we take is guided by His loving hand.

Day 14 - Protection from Evil

Protection from evil is a prayer that echoes in the hearts of those who walk into danger every day, especially law enforcement officers who put their lives on the line to safeguard their communities. These officers face not only physical threats but also the emotional and spiritual challenges that come with confronting humanity's darker side. The risks they take are constant reminders of the fragility of life and the need for strength that goes beyond their own abilities. In Matthew 6:13, Jesus taught His followers to pray, "And lead us not into temptation, but deliver us from evil: For thine is the kingdom, and the power, and the glory, for ever. Amen," a plea for divine protection and guidance in a world where danger and temptation are ever-present. This prayer is not merely a shield against harm but a request for God's presence and power to stand against the forces that seek to disrupt, harm, and destroy. Just as officers rely on their training, equipment, and instincts to protect themselves and others, we are called to rely on God's protection and strength to guard us against all forms of evil—both seen and unseen.

Evil manifests in many ways, from the physical dangers officers face on the streets to the spiritual battles that rage within our hearts and minds. For officers, the threats can come in the form of violent encounters, high-stakes emergencies, or the weight of decisions that have life-altering consequences. Yet, these dangers are not limited to physical harm. The stress, fear, and exposure to suffering can take a toll on their mental and emotional well-being, making the need for spiritual protection all the more critical. Similarly, in our daily lives, we encounter challenges that test our faith, temptations that lure us away from God, and adversities that threaten to overwhelm us. Ephesians 6:12 reminds us, "For we wrestle not against flesh and blood, but against principalities, against powers, against the rulers of the darkness of this world, against spiritual wickedness in high *places*." This verse highlights the reality of spiritual warfare, urging us to recognize that the battles we face are not merely physical but deeply spiritual.

Praying for protection from evil is an act of faith and surrender. It is a recognition that we cannot face the challenges of life on our own and that we need God's guidance, strength, and covering to navigate the uncertainties and dangers before us. For officers, this prayer may be whispered at the start of a shift, in the midst of a tense situation, or as they reflect on the events of the day. For all of us, it is a daily reminder to place our trust in God, who is our ultimate protector and deliverer. Psalm 121:7-8 offers this reassurance: "The LORD shall preserve thee from all evil: he shall preserve thy soul. The LORD shall preserve thy going out and thy coming in from this time forth, and even for evermore." These words remind us that God's protection is not limited to physical safety but extends to every aspect of our being—our hearts, minds, and souls.

God's protection does not mean that we will never face danger or hardship, but it does mean that we are never alone in the midst of it. Just as officers rely on their partners and training to stand firm in dangerous situations, we can rely on God's presence and promises to sustain us through life's trials. Isaiah 41:10 reassures us, "Fear thou not; for I *am* with thee: be not dismayed; for I *am* thy God: I will strengthen thee; yea, I will help thee; yea, I will uphold thee with the right hand of my righteousness." This promise is a source of strength and comfort, reminding us that no matter what we face, God is with us, providing the courage and resilience we need to stand firm.

Protection from evil also requires vigilance and preparation. Just as officers train to anticipate and respond to threats, we are called to equip ourselves with the spiritual armor that God provides. Ephesians 6:13-17 outlines the full armor of God, urging us to "Wherefore take unto you the whole armour of God, that ye may be able to withstand in the evil day, and having done all, to stand. Stand therefore, having your loins girt about with truth, and having on the breastplate of righteousness; And your feet shod with the preparation of the gospel of peace; Above all, taking the shield of faith, wherewith ye shall be able to quench all the fiery darts of the wicked. And take the helmet of salvation, and the sword of the Spirit, which is the word of God:" This armor—truth, righteousness, the gospel of peace, faith, salvation, and the Word of God—enables us to stand strong against the attacks of the enemy, guarding our hearts and minds against fear, doubt, and temptation. By staying rooted in God's truth and relying on His strength, we can face the challenges of life with confidence and peace.

Praying for protection from evil is not just about asking for safety; it is about aligning our hearts with God's will and trusting in His sovereignty. It is about recognizing that He is our refuge and fortress, the One who goes before us, walks beside us, and guards us from behind. Psalm 91:1-2 declares, "He that dwelleth in the secret place of the most High shall abide under the shadow of the Almighty. I will say of the LORD, He is my refuge and my fortress: my God; in him will I trust." This assurance invites us to find rest and security in God's presence, even when the world around us feels uncertain and chaotic.

For law enforcement officers, the prayer for protection from evil is deeply personal, a plea for safety not only for themselves but also for their colleagues, families, and the communities they serve. It is a recognition of the risks they face and a declaration of their dependence on God to guide and protect them. For all of us, this prayer is a reminder of our own vulnerability and our need for God's grace and strength to navigate the challenges of life. It is a declaration of faith in His power to deliver us from the snares of the enemy and to lead us into His peace.

Protection from evil also extends beyond ourselves. As we pray for God's protection, we are called to intercede for others, lifting up our families, friends, and communities in prayer. Just as officers work to protect the vulnerable and uphold justice, we are called to be advocates for those who cannot protect themselves, to stand in the gap through prayer and action, and to reflect God's love and compassion in a broken world. Philippians 4:6-7 encourages us, "Be careful for nothing; but in every thing by prayer and supplication with thanksgiving let your requests be made known unto God. And the peace of God, which passeth all understanding, shall keep your hearts and minds through Christ Jesus." This peace, born of trust and prayer, enables us to face life's challenges with confidence and hope, knowing that God is our protector and provider.

Ultimately, the prayer for protection from evil is a declaration of our trust in God's goodness and power. It is a reminder that He is greater than any threat we face, that His plans for us are good, and that His love is unshakable. As we pray, "Deliver us from evil," we are placing our lives in His hands, trusting that He will guide us, sustain us, and protect us from harm. Whether we face physical dangers, spiritual battles, or the uncertainties of life, we can find peace in the knowledge that God is our refuge and strength, "To the chief Musician for the sons of Korah, A Song upon Alamoth.) God *is* our refuge and strength, a very present help in trouble. (Psalm 46:1). May we walk each day with the confidence that comes from His protection, living as testimonies to His faithfulness and love, and sharing His peace with a world in need.

Day 15 - Provision in Need

Provision in need is a truth that brings hope and assurance to everyone who faces moments of uncertainty, whether in the line of duty or in the everyday struggles of life. For law enforcement officers, having the right resources—equipment, training, and support—is essential to their work. They rely on these provisions to navigate high-pressure situations, protect their communities, and ensure their own safety. Similarly, in our spiritual journey, we rely on God's provision to sustain us, guide us, and meet our needs in ways that go beyond what we can achieve on our own. Philippians 4:19 reminds us of this powerful promise: "But my God shall supply all your need according to his riches in glory by Christ Jesus." These words are a comforting reminder that God, in His infinite love and wisdom, knows our every need and is faithful to provide for us in every circumstance, whether physical, emotional, or spiritual.

For officers, the importance of provision is clear in their daily work. They need protective gear to shield them from harm, reliable communication tools to coordinate their efforts, and the knowledge and skills to make quick, informed decisions. Without these resources, their ability to serve and protect would be compromised. In the same way, we need God's provision to face the challenges of life, from the material necessities that sustain us to the strength and wisdom that enable us to persevere. Just as officers trust their training and equipment to support them in critical moments, we are called to trust in God's promise to provide for our every need, knowing that His resources are limitless and His timing is perfect.

God's provision is not always what we expect, but it is always exactly what we need. Sometimes, His provision comes in the form of tangible blessings—food, shelter, finances, or opportunities. Other times, it is less visible but just as vital: peace in the midst of chaos, strength in the face of adversity, or the presence of a supportive friend during a difficult season. In each instance, God's provision reminds us of His faithfulness and care, showing us that we are never alone and that He is intimately involved in every detail of our lives. Matthew 6:31-33 assures us, "Therefore take no thought, saying, What shall we eat? or, What shall we drink? or, Wherewithal shall we be clothed? For after all these things do the Gentiles seek:) for your heavenly Father knoweth that ye have need of all these things. But seek ye first the kingdom of God, and his righteousness; and all these things shall be added unto you." This passage calls us to prioritize our relationship with God, trusting that He will meet our needs as we align our lives with His will.

Provision in need also teaches us to depend on God rather than ourselves. In a culture that often values self-reliance and independence, it can be challenging to admit that we cannot do it all on our own. Yet, acknowledging our need for God's provision is not a sign of weakness; it is a recognition of His greatness and our reliance on His grace. Just as officers work as part of a team, relying on their colleagues for support and collaboration, we are called to rely on God and His provision, trusting that He will supply what we lack and guide us through every situation. Proverbs 3:5-6 encourages us, "Trust in the LORD with all thine heart; and lean not unto thine own understanding. In all thy ways acknowledge him, and he shall direct thy paths." This trust allows us to release our worries and rest in the assurance that God is in control.

God's provision is often revealed through the people and opportunities He places in our lives. Just as officers benefit from the support of their teams, families, and communities, we experience God's provision through the kindness, generosity, and encouragement of others. Whether it's a friend offering a listening ear, a mentor sharing wisdom, or a stranger extending a helping hand, these moments remind us of God's care and the ways He uses His people to meet our needs. Galatians 6:2 calls us to "Trust in the LORD with all thine heart; and lean not unto thine own understanding. In all thy ways acknowledge him, and he shall direct thy paths." By sharing our resources, time, and love with others, we not only reflect God's provision but also become part of His plan to care for His children.

Provision in need also requires patience and faith. There are times when God's provision does not come immediately or in the way we expect. In these moments, it can be tempting to doubt His faithfulness or to try to take matters into our own hands. Yet, Scripture reminds us that God's timing is always perfect and that His plans for us are good. Isaiah 40:31 offers this encouragement: "But they that wait upon the LORD shall renew *their* strength; they shall mount up with wings as eagles; they shall run, and not be weary; *and* they shall walk, and not faint." Waiting on God's provision is not a passive act; it is an active expression of trust, a declaration of faith that He will provide exactly what we need at exactly the right time.

For law enforcement officers, provision in need is both a practical and spiritual reality. They rely on the tangible resources that enable them to do their jobs effectively, but they also rely on God's strength, wisdom, and protection to navigate the challenges they face. In the same way, we are called to trust in God's provision for every aspect of our lives, from our daily needs to our deepest longings. This trust frees us from the burden of worry and allows us to live with confidence and peace, knowing that our heavenly Father is always faithful to provide.

God's provision is not limited to meeting our immediate needs; it also equips us to fulfill His purpose for our lives. Just as officers rely on their training and resources to carry out their mission, we are equipped by God with the gifts, talents, and opportunities we need to serve Him and others. Ephesians 2:10 reminds us, "For we are his workmanship, created in Christ Jesus unto good works, which God hath before ordained that we should walk in them." This truth encourages us to see God's provision not only as a blessing but also as a responsibility, a call to use what He has given us to glorify Him and to make a difference in the lives of others.

Ultimately, provision in need is a reflection of God's character—His love, faithfulness, and generosity. It is a reminder that He is not only aware of our needs but also deeply committed to meeting them, often in ways that exceed our expectations. As we experience His provision, we are invited to respond with gratitude, worship, and a willingness to share His blessings with others. Philippians 4:6-7 encourages us, "Be careful for nothing; but in every thing by prayer and supplication with thanksgiving let your requests be made known unto God. And the peace of God, which passeth all understanding, shall keep your hearts and minds through Christ Jesus." This peace, born of trust in God's provision, enables us to face life's challenges with confidence and hope.

In every season, whether in abundance or in need, may we remember that God is our ultimate provider. Just as officers trust in their resources to guide them through their work, we can trust in God's provision to sustain us, strengthen us, and lead us forward. Let us live with hearts full of gratitude, faith, and generosity, knowing that His provision is always enough and that He is faithful to supply all our needs according to His riches in glory by Christ Jesus.

Day 16 - Purity of Heart

Purity of heart is a calling that goes beyond outward actions—it is about the integrity, sincerity, and alignment of our inner lives with God's will. For law enforcement officers, integrity is the cornerstone of their work. Every decision they make, every word they speak, and every action they take must reflect their commitment to justice, fairness, and service. Their integrity earns the trust of their communities and strengthens the bonds that hold society together. Similarly, in our spiritual journey, purity of heart is essential. It means living with honesty, humility, and devotion to God, allowing our motives, thoughts, and desires to be shaped by His truth. Jesus said in Matthew 5:8, "Blessed *are* the pure in heart: for they shall see God." This promise reminds us that purity of heart is not just about moral behavior but about a deeper connection with God, a relationship built on trust, transparency, and love. It is a call to live authentically, to seek His presence above all else, and to reflect His character in every aspect of our lives.

For officers, maintaining integrity requires vigilance and dedication. It means resisting the temptation to take shortcuts, to act out of self-interest, or to compromise their values in difficult situations. It means holding themselves accountable and striving to do what is right, even when no one is watching. This commitment to integrity mirrors the pursuit of purity of heart in our spiritual lives. Just as officers are called to act with honor, we are called to align our hearts with God's righteousness, to let go of anything that hinders our relationship with Him, and to live in a way that honors His name. Psalm 24:3-4 asks, "Who shall ascend into the hill of the LORD? or who shall stand in his holy place? He that hath clean hands, and a pure heart; who hath not lifted up his soul unto vanity, nor sworn deceitfully." This verse challenges us to examine our lives, to seek forgiveness for our shortcomings, and to allow God to cleanse us from within.

Purity of heart is not about perfection; it is about intention. It is about seeking God with a sincere desire to know Him, love Him, and follow Him. In a world that often prioritizes appearances over authenticity, this pursuit requires courage and humility. It means acknowledging our weaknesses, admitting our mistakes, and asking God to transform us from the inside out.

Just as officers must constantly evaluate their actions and motives to ensure they are upholding their oath, we must examine our hearts regularly, asking God to reveal anything that does not align with His will. Psalm 51:10 is a powerful prayer for this process: "Create in me a clean heart, O God; and renew a right spirit within me." This prayer invites God to purify our hearts, to fill us with His Spirit, and to guide us in living a life that reflects His holiness.

The pursuit of purity of heart also requires us to guard against the influences that can corrupt our thoughts, desires, and actions. For officers, this might mean resisting the cynicism that can come from witnessing humanity's flaws or maintaining professional boundaries that protect their integrity. For believers, it means being mindful of what we allow into our hearts and minds—whether through the media we consume, the relationships we nurture, or the choices we make. Proverbs 4:23 warns, "Keep thy heart with all diligence; for out of it *are* the issues of life." This verse reminds us that our hearts are the wellspring of our actions and attitudes, and that guarding them is essential for living a life of purity and purpose.

Purity of heart is also about our relationships with others. Just as officers build trust through honesty, fairness, and respect, we are called to interact with others in a way that reflects God's love and truth. This means treating people with kindness, speaking with sincerity, and acting with integrity in all our dealings. It means letting go of bitterness, envy, or deceit, and choosing instead to love, forgive, and serve as Christ did. Ephesians 4:31-32 encourages us, "Let all bitterness, and wrath, and anger, and clamour, and evil speaking, be put away from you, with all malice: And be ye kind one to another, tenderhearted, forgiving one another, even as God for Christ's sake hath forgiven you." These words remind us that purity of heart is not just about our relationship with God but also about how we reflect His character in our relationships with others.

The pursuit of purity of heart is not easy, but it is deeply rewarding. Jesus's promise in Matthew 5:8—"Blessed are the pure in heart: for they shall see God"—speaks to the profound joy and peace that come from living in alignment with His will. When our hearts are pure, we are able to see God more clearly—not just in the sense of eternal life but in our daily lives, as we recognize His presence, hear His voice, and experience His guidance. Purity of heart allows us to walk in close fellowship with Him, to find comfort in His love, and to trust in His plan, even when life feels uncertain or difficult.

Maintaining purity of heart also requires reliance on God's grace. Just as officers depend on their training, equipment, and team to uphold their integrity in challenging situations, we must depend on God's strength to help us stay true to His calling. We cannot achieve purity of heart on our own; it is a work of the Holy Spirit within us, transforming us from the inside out. Philippians 1:6 reminds us, "Being confident of this very thing, that he which hath begun a good work in you will perform *it* until the day of Jesus Christ:" This promise assures us that God is faithful to complete the work He has started in us, to purify our hearts, and to lead us into a deeper relationship with Him.

Ultimately, purity of heart is about living a life that reflects God's holiness and love. It is about choosing to follow Him wholeheartedly, to let go of anything that hinders our relationship with Him, and to allow His truth to shape every aspect of our lives. It is about seeking His presence, trusting in His grace, and walking in His ways, knowing that He is faithful to guide us, sustain us, and bless us as we pursue Him. May we strive each day to live with purity of heart, honoring God in all we do, and finding joy in the promise that those who are pure in heart shall see Him.

Day 17 - Pardon and Forgiveness

Pardon and forgiveness stand as two of the most powerful expressions of love and grace, and they carry profound significance both in the pursuit of justice and in the practice of faith. For law enforcement officers, the pursuit of justice is at the core of their calling, requiring them to uphold laws, seek truth, and ensure that accountability is met. Yet even as officers work tirelessly to maintain order and protect their communities, they often witness the complex realities of human behavior—acts of brokenness, choices born out of desperation, and moments when mercy, not judgment, is the key to healing. In this tension between justice and mercy, we are reminded of God's boundless grace and His command to forgive. Jesus's words in Luke 6:37, "Judge not, and ye shall not be judged: condemn not, and ye shall not be condemned: forgive, and ye shall be forgiven:" challenge us to embrace the transformative power of forgiveness, recognizing that just as we have been pardoned by God, we are called to extend that same mercy to others. Forgiveness is not about condoning wrongdoing; it is about releasing the hold of bitterness and allowing God's love to restore what has been broken.

For officers, pardon and forgiveness may seem at odds with the responsibilities of their role, yet they are deeply intertwined. While justice seeks accountability, forgiveness seeks restoration, offering an opportunity for redemption and renewal. Officers often encounter individuals at their lowest moments—those who have made mistakes, hurt others, or strayed from the path of righteousness. In these encounters, the power of forgiveness becomes evident, not as a replacement for justice but as a complement to it. Forgiveness acknowledges the humanity of those who have erred, offering them a chance to change and reminding them that their mistakes do not define their worth. Similarly, in our spiritual lives, forgiveness is an act of grace that reflects God's character and allows us to live in the freedom of His mercy. Ephesians 4:32 encourages us, "And be ye kind one to another, tenderhearted, forgiving one another, even as God for Christ's sake hath forgiven you." This verse reminds us that forgiveness is not just a gift we give to others but a response to the forgiveness we have already received.

Forgiveness is a cornerstone of faith because it mirrors God's relationship with us. In His infinite mercy, God offers us pardon for our sins, wiping away our guilt and giving us a new beginning. This divine forgiveness is not something we can earn or deserve; it is a gift, freely given through the sacrifice of Jesus Christ. Romans 5:8 declares, "But God commendeth his love toward us, in that, while we were yet sinners, Christ died for us." This truth is a powerful reminder of the depth of God's love and the extent of His grace. Just as He has forgiven us, He calls us to extend that forgiveness to others, breaking the cycle of resentment and allowing His peace to reign in our hearts.

However, forgiveness is not always easy. Whether we are forgiving others, seeking forgiveness for ourselves, or grappling with the need to forgive the injustices we see in the world, the process can be challenging and deeply personal. Forgiveness requires humility, courage, and a willingness to let go of anger, hurt, and pride. It means choosing to release the burden of grudges and to trust God with the outcomes, knowing that He is the ultimate judge and arbiter of justice. Matthew 6:14-15 underscores this truth: "For if ye forgive men their trespasses, your heavenly Father will also forgive you: But if ye forgive not men their trespasses, neither will your Father forgive your trespasses." This passage reminds us that forgiveness is not optional; it is a command that reflects our understanding of God's grace and our willingness to live in obedience to Him.

Forgiveness is also a gift we give to ourselves. Holding onto resentment and bitterness weighs heavily on our hearts, creating barriers to joy, peace, and spiritual growth. For officers, the emotional toll of their work can be immense, often leaving them grappling with anger, frustration, or sorrow over the injustices they witness. In these moments, forgiveness becomes a path to healing, allowing them to release the emotional burdens they carry and to find solace in God's presence. Similarly, in our own lives, forgiveness frees us from the chains of past hurts, enabling us to move forward with a renewed sense of hope and purpose. Colossians 3:13 urges us, "Forbearing one another, and forgiving one another, if any man have a quarrel against any: even as Christ forgave you, so also *do* ye." By choosing forgiveness, we align our hearts with God's will and open ourselves to the transformative power of His love.

Forgiveness is not about ignoring the consequences of wrongdoing or pretending that pain does not exist. It is about acknowledging the reality of what has happened while choosing to respond with grace rather than vengeance. It is about recognizing that true justice is rooted in God's righteousness, not in our own desire for retribution. Micah 6:8 offers a profound reminder of this balance: "He hath shewed thee, O man, what *is* good; and what doth the LORD require of thee, but to do justly, and to love mercy, and to walk humbly with thy God?" This verse calls us to pursue justice with a heart of mercy, knowing that forgiveness and accountability can coexist and that both are part of God's redemptive plan.

Forgiveness also extends to ourselves. Just as we are called to forgive others, we must also learn to accept God's forgiveness for our own mistakes and shortcomings. For officers, this might mean releasing the guilt of a decision made under pressure or the regret of not being able to do more in a given situation. For all of us, it means embracing the truth that God's grace is sufficient and that His love covers our imperfections. Psalm 103:12 reassures us, "As far as the east is from the west, *so* far hath he removed our transgressions from us." This promise invites us to let go of self-condemnation and to live in the freedom of God's forgiveness, allowing His mercy to shape our identity and purpose.

Forgiveness is a powerful act of faith that transforms not only relationships but also communities. Just as officers work to rebuild trust and restore peace in the aftermath of conflict, forgiveness has the potential to heal divisions, mend broken relationships, and foster reconciliation. It creates space for dialogue, understanding, and growth, allowing individuals and communities to move forward together. In our spiritual lives, forgiveness is a testimony to God's love, a reflection of His character that draws others closer to Him. Matthew 5:16 encourages us, "Let your light so shine before men, that they may see your good works, and glorify your Father which is in heaven." By choosing forgiveness, we become vessels of God's grace, shining His light into a world that desperately needs it.

Ultimately, pardon and forgiveness are not about ignoring justice but about trusting God to bring about His perfect justice in His perfect time. They are about surrendering our desire for control and allowing His love to guide our actions and attitudes. They are about living in the freedom of His grace and extending that grace to others, knowing that forgiveness is a gift that reflects the heart of God. As we forgive, we open ourselves to His peace, His joy, and His presence, experiencing the fullness of life that He desires for us. May we embrace the call to forgive, trusting in the power of God's mercy to heal, restore, and transform our lives and the lives of those around us.

Day 18 - Preparedness for Action

Preparedness for action is a way of life for law enforcement officers and believers alike, as both are called to face challenges that require readiness, resilience, and determination. For officers, gearing up for duty is a daily ritual that involves more than just donning a uniform or holstering equipment—it is about mentally, physically, and emotionally preparing to confront whatever lies ahead, from routine tasks to high-stakes emergencies. They rely on their training, tools, and instincts to navigate unpredictable and often dangerous situations, knowing that every moment requires vigilance and courage. Similarly, as Christians, we are called to prepare for the spiritual battles we face in life by equipping ourselves with the tools God has provided. Ephesians 6:11 reminds us, "Put on the whole armour of God, that ye may be able to stand against the wiles of the devil." This verse calls us to take action, to be intentional in our faith, and to arm ourselves with God's truth and power so we can stand firm in the face of trials, temptations, and adversity.

For officers, the act of gearing up is second nature. Every piece of equipment they wear serves a specific purpose: a vest to protect against harm, a radio to ensure communication, a badge to represent authority, and tools to de-escalate situations or enforce the law. Each item is essential to their role, and they never step into the field without being fully prepared. In the same way, believers are called to equip themselves with spiritual armor that protects and empowers them in the battles of life. The armor of God, described in Ephesians 6:13-17, includes the belt of truth, the breastplate of righteousness, the shoes of peace, the shield of faith, the helmet of salvation, and the sword of the Spirit. Each piece serves a vital role in our spiritual readiness, ensuring that we are equipped to stand strong against the challenges that come our way.

The belt of truth is the foundation of our armor, just as a belt anchors an officer's gear. Truth provides stability and clarity, helping us navigate a world often clouded by deception and confusion. It reminds us of who God is, who we are in Him, and the promises He has made. The breastplate of righteousness guards our hearts, protecting us from the wounds of guilt, shame, and temptation. It is a reminder to live with integrity and to align our actions with God's will, just as officers strive to act with honor and uphold justice. The shoes of peace enable us to stand firm and move forward with confidence, no matter how unsteady the ground beneath us may feel. They remind us that God's peace is not the absence of conflict but the presence of His assurance, guiding our steps and keeping us steady in the face of uncertainty.

The shield of faith is our defense against the attacks of doubt, fear, and discouragement. Just as an officer's shield provides protection in dangerous situations, our faith shields us from the fiery darts of the enemy, enabling us to trust in God's power and promises even when circumstances seem overwhelming. The helmet of salvation guards our minds, reminding us of the hope we have in Christ and protecting us from the lies that seek to undermine our faith. And finally, the sword of the Spirit, which is the Word of God, is our weapon of truth and power. It equips us to stand against the enemy's schemes, to declare God's promises, and to live boldly for Him.

Preparedness for action requires intentionality and discipline. Just as officers must regularly maintain their equipment, sharpen their skills, and stay physically fit, we must continually invest in our spiritual growth and readiness. This means spending time in God's Word, seeking His presence in prayer, and staying connected to a community of believers who can encourage and support us. Hebrews 10:24-25 reminds us, "And let us consider one another to provoke unto love and to good works: Not forsaking the assembling of ourselves together, as the manner of some is; but exhorting one another: and so much the more, as ye see the day approaching." Spiritual preparedness is not a one-time event but a lifelong commitment to walking with God and relying on His strength.

Preparedness also requires vigilance. Officers are trained to remain alert and aware, constantly assessing their surroundings and anticipating potential risks. As believers, we are called to the same level of vigilance in our spiritual lives. 1 Peter 5:8 warns us, "Be sober, be vigilant; because your adversary the devil, as a roaring lion, walketh about, seeking whom he may devour:" This call to vigilance reminds us that we are in a spiritual battle, and that staying prepared requires us to remain rooted in God's truth and dependent on His power. It means being aware of the enemy's tactics and guarding against complacency, always ready to stand firm in faith and obedience.

Preparedness for action also requires courage. Officers step into situations that demand bravery and resolve, often facing dangers that test their limits.

In the same way, living out our faith requires courage, especially when we encounter opposition, uncertainty, or adversity. Joshua 1:9 offers this encouragement: "Have not I commanded thee? Be strong and of a good courage; be not afraid, neither be thou dismayed: for the LORD thy God *is* with thee whithersoever thou goest." This promise reminds us that our courage comes not from our own strength but from the presence and power of God, who goes before us and fights for us.

Finally, preparedness for action is about purpose. Just as officers gear up with a clear mission to serve and protect, we are called to live with purpose, using the gifts and resources God has given us to advance His kingdom and reflect His love. Ephesians 2:10 reminds us, "For we are his workmanship, created in Christ Jesus unto good works, which God hath before ordained that we should walk in them." Every moment of our lives is an opportunity to live out this purpose, to stand firm in faith, and to make a difference in the lives of those around us.

Ultimately, preparedness for action is about trusting in God's provision and stepping forward with confidence, knowing that He has equipped us for every challenge we will face. As we put on the whole armor of God, we are reminded that we do not fight our battles alone; we are strengthened by His presence, guided by His truth, and empowered by His Spirit. May we live each day with readiness and resolve, standing firm in faith and walking boldly in the purpose God has set before us.

Day 19 - Persistence in Justice

Persistence in justice is both a calling and a responsibility that requires unwavering commitment, courage, and faith. For law enforcement officers, the pursuit of justice is at the very heart of their work. Every case they investigate, every decision they make, and every action they take is guided by their duty to uphold the law, protect the innocent, and ensure that fairness prevails. This mission is not without its challenges. Officers often find themselves navigating complex, high-pressure situations where the lines between right and wrong can feel blurred, and the path to justice is anything but straightforward. Yet, they press on, driven by their conviction that justice is worth fighting for. In the same way, as followers of Christ, we are called to act justly, to pursue what is right, and to reflect God's character in our actions and decisions. Micah 6:8 speaks directly to this calling: "He hath shewed thee, O man, what *is* good; and what doth the LORD require of thee, but to do justly, and to love mercy, and to walk humbly with thy God?" This verse reminds us that justice is not just an abstract ideal but a daily practice, one that requires both determination and humility.

For officers, persistence in justice means staying the course, even when the odds are stacked against them. It means refusing to give up when investigations stall, evidence is scarce, or the weight of the job feels overwhelming. It means standing firm in the face of criticism, doubt, or fear, trusting that their efforts are making a difference, even when the results are not immediately visible. Similarly, in our spiritual lives, persistence in justice requires us to remain faithful to God's calling, even when the challenges we face seem insurmountable. It means standing up for what is right, even when it is unpopular or inconvenient, and choosing to act with integrity, even when no one is watching. Galatians 6:9 encourages us, "And let us not be weary in well doing: for in due season we shall reap, if we faint not." This promise reminds us that our persistence is not in vain and that God's justice will ultimately prevail.

Justice is not just about enforcing laws or ensuring accountability; it is about reflecting God's character and His desire for a world where fairness, compassion, and truth reign. For officers, this means approaching their work with a sense of empathy and respect, recognizing the humanity of those they serve and striving to treat everyone with dignity and fairness. For believers, it means allowing God's love to guide our actions, seeking not only to uphold what is right but also to extend grace and mercy to those who need it most. Zechariah 7:9-10 captures this balance beautifully: "Thus speaketh the LORD of hosts, saying, Execute true judgment, and shew mercy and compassions every man to his brother: And oppress not the widow, nor the fatherless, the stranger, nor the poor; and let none of you imagine evil against his brother in your heart." Justice and mercy are not opposing forces; they are two sides of the same coin, reflecting the heart of God and His desire for reconciliation and restoration.

Persistence in justice also requires us to confront the injustices we see in the world, even when it is uncomfortable or costly. Just as officers step into difficult situations to protect the vulnerable and hold wrongdoers accountable, we are called to be advocates for those who cannot speak for themselves, to challenge systems of oppression, and to stand up for what is right, even when it comes at a personal cost. Proverbs 31:8-9 urges us, "Open thy mouth for the dumb in the cause of all such as are appointed to destruction. Open thy mouth, judge righteously, and plead the cause of the poor and needy." This call to action reminds us that justice is not passive; it requires us to take a stand, to use our voices, and to fight for the dignity and well-being of others.

However, persistence in justice also requires humility. Just as officers must recognize their own limitations and biases, we must approach the pursuit of justice with a heart that is open to God's guidance and correction. Micah 6:8 reminds us that walking humbly with God is an essential part of acting justly and loving mercy. It means acknowledging that we do not have all the answers and that our understanding of justice is incomplete without God's wisdom and truth. It means seeking His perspective, listening to His voice, and allowing His Spirit to shape our hearts and actions. Proverbs 3:5-6 encourages us, "Trust in the LORD with all thine heart; and lean not unto thine own understanding. In all thy ways acknowledge him, and he shall direct thy paths." By relying on God's guidance, we can pursue justice with confidence, knowing that He is leading us in the way of righteousness.

Persistence in justice also requires resilience in the face of setbacks and discouragement. Just as officers must persevere through long hours, difficult cases, and moments of doubt, we must remain steadfast in our commitment to God's calling, even when the results are not immediate or visible. The pursuit of justice is often a long and arduous journey, one that requires patience, perseverance, and an unwavering faith in God's promises. Hebrews 12:1-2 reminds us, "Wherefore seeing we also are compassed about with so great a cloud of witnesses, let us lay aside every weight, and the sin which doth so easily beset us, and let us run with patience the race that is set before us, Looking unto Jesus the author and finisher of our faith; who for the joy that was set before him endured the cross, despising the shame, and is set down at the right hand of the throne of God." This perspective encourages us to keep our eyes on Christ, trusting that He is working through us and that His justice will ultimately prevail.

At its core, persistence in justice is about living out God's love in a broken and hurting world. It is about choosing to see others through His eyes, to act with compassion and integrity, and to reflect His character in all we do. It is about recognizing that justice is not just about punishing wrongdoing but about creating a world where fairness, kindness, and truth can flourish. Isaiah 1:17 calls us to "Learn to do well; seek judgment, relieve the oppressed, judge the fatherless, plead for the widow." This call to action reminds us that justice is not just a concept to be admired but a practice to be lived out in our daily lives.

Ultimately, persistence in justice reflects God's own character. He is a God of justice, who upholds what is right, defends the vulnerable, and brings hope to the oppressed. As His followers, we are called to reflect His heart, to be His hands and feet in the world, and to trust that He is working through us to bring about His kingdom. May we embrace this calling with courage, humility, and faith, knowing that our efforts are not in vain and that God's justice will prevail in the end. Let us persist in the pursuit of justice, loving mercy, and walking humbly with our God, trusting in His promise to guide us, sustain us, and use us for His glory.

Day 20 - Patience with Others

Patience with others is a virtue that speaks to the very heart of love, humility, and understanding. It is the willingness to endure frustration, misunderstandings, or inconvenience without losing composure or kindness. For law enforcement officers, patience is an essential part of their role. Each day, they encounter a diverse range of individuals—some frightened, others angry, confused, or in crisis. They must navigate these interactions with calm and restraint, even when emotions run high or circumstances are tense. Officers learn to listen, empathize, and respond thoughtfully, recognizing that patience often de-escalates conflict and builds trust. Similarly, as believers, we are called to exercise patience in our relationships with others, reflecting the love and grace of God in every interaction. Ephesians 4:2 reminds us to live "With all lowliness and meekness, with longsuffering, forbearing one another in love;" This verse challenges us to approach others with humility, gentleness, and a willingness to endure their imperfections, knowing that we, too, are recipients of God's unending patience.

Patience is not passive; it is an active choice to prioritize understanding over judgment, compassion over frustration, and peace over conflict. For officers, this might mean taking the time to explain a situation to someone who is confused or overwhelmed, responding calmly to hostility, or showing empathy to someone in a difficult circumstance. For us, it might mean extending grace to a coworker who tests our patience, showing kindness to a friend who repeatedly makes mistakes, or refraining from anger when someone wrongs us. Patience requires us to set aside our own pride and desires, focusing instead on the needs and perspective of the other person. Proverbs 15:1 reminds us, "A soft answer turneth away wrath: but grievous words stir up anger." This wisdom highlights the power of patience to diffuse tension and foster understanding, even in the most challenging situations.

Being patient with others often requires us to see beyond their actions to the deeper struggles or fears that may be driving them. Just as officers are trained to recognize that anger or resistance often stems from fear or pain, we are called to look beyond the surface and approach others with empathy and compassion. This perspective helps us respond not with frustration but with kindness, offering support and understanding to those who need it most. Colossians 3:12 encourages us, "Put on therefore, as the elect of God, holy and beloved, bowels of mercies, kindness, humbleness of mind, meekness, longsuffering;" By choosing to be patient, we reflect God's character and create opportunities for healing, growth, and reconciliation.

Patience also involves recognizing our own limitations and relying on God's strength to sustain us. Just as officers face moments when their patience is tested to its limits, we, too, encounter situations that challenge our ability to remain calm and compassionate. In these moments, it is essential to turn to God, asking for His grace to fill us and His Spirit to guide us. Galatians 5:22 lists patience as a fruit of the Spirit, reminding us that it is not something we can manufacture on our own but a quality that God cultivates within us as we draw closer to Him. By staying connected to His presence, we can respond to others with the same patience and love that He has shown to us.

Patience with others is also an act of humility. It requires us to let go of the need to be right, the desire for control, and the impulse to assert our own will. Instead, it calls us to listen, to learn, and to prioritize the well-being of others. Philippians 2:3-4 challenges us, "Let nothing be done through strife or vainglory; but in lowliness of mind let each esteem other better than themselves. Look not every man on his own things, but every man also on the things of others." This humility allows us to approach others with an open heart, ready to extend grace and understanding rather than judgment or impatience.

Patience is especially important in moments of conflict or misunderstanding. Just as officers must remain calm and composed when facing hostility or resistance, we are called to respond to conflict with gentleness and self-control. James 1:19 advises, "Wherefore, my beloved brethren, let every man be swift to hear, slow to speak, slow to wrath:" By taking the time to listen and consider the perspective of others, we can avoid misunderstandings and work toward resolution rather than escalation. Patience allows us to create space for dialogue, to build bridges rather than walls, and to foster relationships that are grounded in mutual respect and love.

However, patience does not mean tolerating harm or enabling wrongdoing. Just as officers must balance patience with the need to enforce justice and maintain safety, we must discern when to extend grace and when to set boundaries. Patience is not about ignoring issues or avoiding confrontation; it is about addressing challenges with a spirit of love and a desire for restoration. Ephesians 4:15 reminds us to speak the truth in love, growing in maturity and unity as we navigate the complexities of our relationships. This balance of patience and truth ensures that our interactions are both compassionate and constructive, reflecting God's wisdom and grace.

Ultimately, patience with others is rooted in our understanding of God's patience with us. Despite our flaws, failures, and repeated mistakes, God remains steadfast in His love, extending forgiveness and grace time and again. 2 Peter 3:9 beautifully illustrates this truth: "The Lord is not slack concerning his promise, as some men count slackness; but is longsuffering to us-ward, not willing that any should perish, but that all should come to repentance." God's patience is a model for how we are called to treat others, reminding us that just as He has been patient with us, we must be patient with those around us.

By choosing patience, we create opportunities for growth, healing, and connection. Whether it's a tense moment that requires a calm response, a difficult relationship that calls for perseverance, or a challenging situation that demands empathy, patience allows us to reflect God's love in tangible ways. It transforms our interactions, softens our hearts, and fosters an environment where grace and understanding can flourish. May we strive to live "with all lowliness and meekness, with longsuffering," as Ephesians 4:2 instructs, showing patience to all we encounter and glorifying God through our love and kindness.

Day 21 - Promoting Peace

Promoting peace is a calling that resonates deeply in the heart of every community, every relationship, and every life touched by the challenges of discord. For law enforcement officers, the pursuit of peace is central to their mission. Each day, they step into situations of conflict, fear, or uncertainty, striving to de-escalate tensions, restore order, and create an environment where individuals can feel safe and valued. Whether mediating disputes, protecting the vulnerable, or simply being a calm presence in times of chaos, officers work tirelessly to promote peace, knowing that their efforts have the power to transform lives. In the same way, we are called as followers of Christ to be peacemakers in our relationships and communities, reflecting His love and grace through our words and actions. Psalm 34:14 commands us, "Depart from evil, and do good; seek peace, and pursue it." This verse reminds us that peace is not passive—it is something we actively seek, pursue, and cultivate, even in the face of challenges and opposition.

Promoting peace requires intentionality and courage. For officers, this might mean stepping into volatile situations, listening to opposing sides, and making decisions that prioritize safety and fairness. For us, it means being willing to set aside our own pride, anger, or desires to foster understanding, reconciliation, and harmony in our relationships. Promoting peace involves choosing our words carefully, approaching others with humility, and seeking solutions that honor God and uplift those around us. Proverbs 15:1 reminds us, "A soft answer turneth away wrath: but grievous words stir up anger." This wisdom highlights the power of gentleness and kindness to diffuse conflict and create opportunities for healing.

Being a peacemaker also requires us to address the root causes of discord rather than simply treating the symptoms. Just as officers work to understand the underlying issues behind a conflict, we are called to look beyond surface-level disagreements and seek deeper understanding. This might mean listening to someone's perspective without judgment, acknowledging their feelings, and being willing to forgive and seek forgiveness. Ephesians 4:3 encourages us, "Endeavouring to keep the unity of the Spirit in the bond of peace." Unity and peace go hand in hand, and fostering them often requires us to put aside our own agendas and work together for the greater good.

Promoting peace also involves standing up against injustice. Just as officers protect the vulnerable and defend the rights of those who cannot defend themselves, we are called to be advocates for fairness, compassion, and dignity in our communities. Micah 6:8 reminds us of this dual calling: "He hath shewed thee, O man, what *is* good; and what doth the LORD require of thee, but to do justly, and to love mercy, and to walk humbly with thy God?" True peace is not the absence of conflict but the presence of justice and righteousness. By addressing issues of inequality, prejudice, or oppression, we help create an environment where peace can flourish, reflecting God's kingdom here on earth.

At its core, promoting peace is about reflecting the character of Christ. Jesus Himself is called the Prince of Peace, and His life and teachings provide the ultimate example of what it means to be a peacemaker. In Matthew 5:9, Jesus declares, "Blessed *are* the peacemakers: for they shall be called the children of God." This blessing emphasizes the importance of seeking peace as a way of living out our identity as God's children. By following Christ's example, we can approach conflicts with grace, extend forgiveness to those who wrong us, and build bridges of understanding in a world that often feels divided and fragmented.

Promoting peace also requires perseverance. Just as officers face challenges, setbacks, and resistance in their efforts to maintain peace, we, too, will encounter obstacles in our pursuit of harmony. There will be times when our efforts are met with hostility, when reconciliation feels impossible, or when the divisions around us seem too great to overcome. In these moments, it is essential to remember that peace is a journey, not a destination. Galatians 6:9 encourages us, "And let us not be weary in well doing: for in due season we shall reap, if we faint not." By staying faithful to the call to promote peace, we can trust that God is working through us to bring about His purpose, even when the results are not immediately visible.

Being a peacemaker also means fostering peace within ourselves. Just as officers must remain calm and composed in high-pressure situations, we are called to cultivate an inner peace that allows us to approach life's challenges with confidence and faith. Philippians 4:6-7 offers this assurance: "Be careful for nothing; but in every thing by prayer and supplication with thanksgiving let your requests be made known unto God. And the peace of God, which passeth all understanding, shall keep your hearts and minds through Christ Jesus." This inner peace, born of trust in God's presence and provision, enables us to be a steady and reassuring presence for others, even in times of uncertainty or conflict.

Promoting peace also involves creating environments where relationships can thrive. Just as officers work to build trust and cooperation within their communities, we are called to foster connections that are grounded in love, respect, and mutual understanding. Romans 12:18 challenges us, "If it be possible, as much as lieth in you, live peaceably with all men." This call to live at peace with others requires us to be intentional about resolving conflicts, addressing misunderstandings, and prioritizing reconciliation over division.

Ultimately, promoting peace is about pointing others to the ultimate source of peace—Jesus Christ. True and lasting peace cannot be achieved through human efforts alone; it is a gift from God that transforms hearts, heals wounds, and restores relationships. By sharing the message of Christ's love and forgiveness, we invite others to experience the peace that only He can provide. Isaiah 26:3 declares, "Thou wilt keep *him* in perfect peace, *whose* mind *is* stayed *on thee*: because he trusteth in thee." As we keep our focus on God and trust in His promises, we can become instruments of His peace, bringing hope and healing to a world in need.

Promoting peace is both a privilege and a responsibility. Whether through small acts of kindness, courageous stands for justice, or quiet moments of understanding, every effort we make to seek peace reflects the heart of God and advances His kingdom. May we embrace this calling with humility, determination, and faith, knowing that our efforts are not in vain and that God's peace has the power to transform lives, communities, and the world. Let us "depart from evil, and do good; seek peace, and pursue it," living as peacemakers who bring glory to God and shine His light in the darkest places.

Day 22 - Protection through Prayer

Protection through prayer is a powerful and unshakable source of strength, guidance, and peace, offering a lifeline to all who face challenges, uncertainty, or danger. For law enforcement officers, the dangers of the job are both visible and unseen, from high-stakes situations to the emotional toll of constant vigilance. While officers rely on their training, equipment, and the support of their teams to stay safe, many also recognize the necessity of something deeper: the protective power of prayer. Prayer becomes a shield, a source of courage, and a way to find clarity and calm in the midst of chaos. In the same way, as believers, we are called to rely on constant prayer as our connection to God—a lifeline that grounds us, equips us, and surrounds us with His protection. The apostle Paul's exhortation in 1 Thessalonians 5:17 to "pray without ceasing" reminds us that prayer is not an occasional act but an ongoing relationship with the One who knows us, loves us, and watches over us at all times.

For officers, support from their communities, families, and colleagues is crucial, but even more essential is the spiritual support found through prayer. When they step into unpredictable situations, prayer serves as a reminder that they are not alone—that God is with them, guiding their steps, protecting their hearts, and strengthening their resolve. Similarly, in our daily lives, we face spiritual battles that require the constant protection and provision of God's presence. Prayer is how we invite Him into every moment, asking for His wisdom when decisions are tough, His peace when fears arise, and His protection when dangers loom. Psalm 91:2-4 offers this assurance: "I will say of the LORD, He is my refuge and my fortress: my God; in him will I trust. Surely he shall deliver thee from the snare of the fowler, and from the noisome pestilence. He shall cover thee with his feathers, and under his wings shalt thou trust: his truth shall be thy shield and buckler." These words remind us that God's protection through prayer is both personal and powerful, a refuge in every storm.

Prayer is not just a request for protection; it is a source of strength and alignment with God's will. Just as officers prepare for their shifts by equipping themselves with the tools they need to face the day, we prepare for life's challenges by turning to God in prayer, asking Him to equip us with His wisdom, courage, and grace. Philippians 4:6-7 encourages us, "Be careful for nothing; but in every thing by prayer and supplication with thanksgiving let your requests be made known unto God. And the peace of God, which passeth all understanding, shall keep your hearts and minds through Christ Jesus.." This promise of peace, born from prayer, sustains us in moments of uncertainty and allows us to face life's trials with calm assurance.

Through prayer, we find clarity when life feels confusing or overwhelming. Officers often have to make split-second decisions that carry significant consequences, relying on both their training and their instincts. For us, prayer serves as a compass, aligning our thoughts and actions with God's purpose and helping us discern the right path when faced with difficult choices. Proverbs 3:5-6 reminds us, "Trust in the LORD with all thine heart; and lean not unto thine own understanding. In all thy ways acknowledge him, and he shall direct thy paths." Prayer is how we surrender our plans to God and trust in His perfect wisdom, knowing that He will guide us with love and faithfulness.

The protection of prayer is not limited to ourselves; it extends to those we intercede for. Just as officers rely on the prayers of their families and communities, we are called to lift others up in prayer, asking God to protect, bless, and strengthen them. Whether we are praying for loved ones, leaders, or those in need, our prayers have the power to bring God's presence into their lives in transformative ways. James 5:16 emphasizes this truth: "Confess *your* faults one to another, and pray one for another, that ye may be healed. The effectual fervent prayer of a righteous man availeth much." Through prayer, we become partners in God's work, interceding on behalf of others and joining Him in bringing His love and protection to the world.

Prayer also protects us from the spiritual battles we face daily. Just as officers are trained to be vigilant and prepared, we are called to stay alert to the challenges and temptations that threaten our faith. Ephesians 6:11-18 speaks of the armor of God, urging us to "Put on the whole armour of God, that ye may be able to stand against the wiles of the devil. For we wrestle not against flesh and blood, but against principalities, against powers, against the rulers of the darkness of this world, against spiritual wickedness in high places. Wherefore take unto you the whole armour of God, that ye may be able to withstand in the evil day, and having done all, to stand. Stand therefore, having your loins girt about with truth, and having on the breastplate of righteousness; And your feet shod with the preparation of the gospel of peace; Above all, taking the shield of faith, wherewith ye shall be able to quench all the fiery darts of the wicked. And take the helmet of salvation, and the sword of the Spirit, which is the word of God: Praying always with all prayer and supplication in the

Spirit, and watching thereunto with all perseverance and supplication for all saints;" Prayer is a vital part of this armor, enabling us to stand firm against fear, doubt, and discouragement. By staying connected to God through prayer, we are fortified with His strength, shielded by His grace, and empowered to overcome whatever comes our way.

One of the most beautiful aspects of prayer is its accessibility. Just as officers carry their radios to maintain constant communication with their teams, we have the gift of prayer as a way to remain in constant communication with God. There are no barriers, no waiting periods—God is always available, ready to hear our prayers and respond with love. Whether we are whispering a quick plea for help in a moment of need or spending quiet time in reflection and thanksgiving, our prayers draw us closer to Him and remind us of His nearness. Psalm 145:18 declares, "The LORD *is* nigh unto all them that call upon him, to all that call upon him in truth." This closeness is a source of comfort and reassurance, reminding us that we are never alone.

Prayer also transforms our hearts, helping us see the world through God's eyes and respond to others with His love and compassion. Just as officers must approach their work with empathy and understanding, we are called to let prayer shape our interactions with others, allowing us to extend grace, forgiveness, and kindness even in challenging situations. Colossians 4:2 encourages us, "Continue in prayer, and watch in the same with thanksgiving;" By making prayer a consistent part of our lives, we cultivate an attitude of gratitude and a heart that reflects God's character.

Ultimately, protection through prayer is a reflection of God's love for us. He invites us to come to Him with our fears, needs, and desires, promising to be our refuge and strength in every circumstance. Isaiah 41:10 offers this reassurance: "Fear thou not; for I *am* with thee: be not dismayed; for I *am* thy God: I will strengthen thee; yea, I will help thee; yea, I will uphold thee with the right hand of my righteousness." This promise reminds us that God's protection is not just about shielding us from harm but about empowering us to face life's challenges with faith and confidence.

As we rely on prayer for protection, let us also remember to give thanks for the ways God has already provided for us. Gratitude strengthens our faith, reminding us of His faithfulness and encouraging us to trust Him with every aspect of our lives. Psalm 100:4 invites us to "Enter into his gates with thanksgiving, *and* into his courts with praise: be thankful unto him, *and* bless his name." Through prayer, we not only seek God's protection but also celebrate His goodness, drawing closer to Him in love and worship.

In every moment, whether in times of danger, uncertainty, or peace, prayer remains our greatest source of protection and strength. Just as officers prepare for their shifts with the tools and support they need, we can approach each day with confidence, knowing that through prayer, we are equipped, guided, and surrounded by the presence of God. Let us embrace the call to "pray without ceasing," trusting in the power of prayer to sustain us, protect us, and draw us closer to the One who holds us in His hands.

Day 23 - Power of Compassion

The power of compassion is a force that transcends words and transforms lives, bringing light to the darkest places and hope to the most broken hearts. For law enforcement officers, compassion is an essential part of their duty, woven into every act of service and every interaction. Whether calming a frightened child, offering comfort to someone in crisis, or simply listening with empathy to a person in need, officers demonstrate the profound impact of kindness in a world often filled with hardship and pain. Similarly, as followers of Christ, we are called to embody compassion in our daily lives, reflecting His love through our words, actions, and attitudes. Ephesians 4:32 urges us, "And be ye kind one to another, tenderhearted, forgiving one another, even as God for Christ's sake hath forgiven you." This verse reminds us that compassion is not just a nice gesture but a fundamental expression of God's character—a reflection of His love, mercy, and grace.

Compassion begins with seeing others through the eyes of Christ. Just as officers encounter people in vulnerable moments, we are surrounded by individuals who are hurting, struggling, or in need of encouragement. Compassion calls us to look beyond outward appearances and into the hearts of others, recognizing their inherent worth and dignity as creations of God. It requires us to set aside our judgments and assumptions, choosing instead to approach each person with kindness and understanding. Colossians 3:12 encourages us, "Put on therefore, as the elect of God, holy and beloved, bowels of mercies, kindness, humbleness of mind, meekness, longsuffering;" This call to action reminds us that compassion is a deliberate choice, a daily commitment to reflect God's love in every interaction.

For officers, compassion is often what de-escalates a tense situation or bridges the gap between authority and community. A kind word, a patient ear, or a gentle demeanor can transform conflict into cooperation and fear into trust. In the same way, our compassion as believers has the power to mend relationships, heal wounds, and foster connection. Proverbs 15:1 highlights this truth: "A soft answer turneth away wrath: but grievous words stir up anger." The way we choose to respond to others—especially in moments of tension—can either inflame division or pave the way for reconciliation.

Compassionate responses diffuse anger and create space for understanding, reminding others that they are valued and loved.

Compassion also involves action. Just as officers go beyond their call of duty to meet the needs of those they serve, we are called to act on our empathy, offering practical help and support to those who are struggling. Whether it's providing for physical needs, offering emotional encouragement, or simply being present with someone in their pain, acts of compassion have the power to change lives. James 2:15-17 challenges us, "If a brother or sister be naked, and destitute of daily food, And one of you say unto them, Depart in peace, be ye warmed and filled; notwithstanding ye give them not those things which are needful to the body; what doth it profit? Even so faith, if it hath not works, is dead, being alone." True compassion moves beyond words and into deeds, demonstrating our faith through tangible expressions of love.

The power of compassion lies in its ability to reflect God's character and draw others closer to Him. Just as officers serve as a visible reminder of protection and care, our compassion points others to the love and mercy of Christ. When we choose to be kind, tenderhearted, and forgiving, we become living testimonies of God's grace, showing the world what it means to be His hands and feet. Matthew 5:16 encourages us, "Let your light so shine before men, that they may see your good works, and glorify your Father which is in heaven." Through acts of compassion, we not only meet immediate needs but also plant seeds of hope, faith, and transformation in the lives of those we encounter.

Compassion also requires humility. Just as officers must approach their work with a willingness to listen and learn, we are called to serve others with a heart of humility, placing their needs above our own. Philippians 2:3-4 exhorts us, "Let nothing be done through strife or vainglory; but in lowliness of mind let each esteem other better than themselves. Look not every man on his own things, but every man also on the things of others." This humility allows us to empathize with others, to share in their joys and sorrows, and to offer our support without seeking recognition or reward.

At times, compassion may feel difficult or even costly. Just as officers face emotional and physical challenges in their efforts to help others, we may encounter resistance, exhaustion, or disappointment in our acts of kindness. Yet, Scripture reminds us that compassion is worth the cost and that God's strength sustains us in our efforts. Galatians 6:9 encourages us, "And let us not be weary in well doing: for in due season we shall reap, if we faint not." By persevering in compassion, we reflect God's unchanging love and trust that He is working through us to bring healing and hope to a hurting world.

Compassion also brings healing to our own hearts. Just as officers find fulfillment and purpose in serving their communities, we experience joy and peace when we extend kindness to others. Acts of compassion draw us closer to God, allowing His love to flow through us and reminding us of the interconnectedness of His creation. Proverbs 11:25 declares, "The liberal soul shall be made fat: and he that watereth shall be watered also himself." When we give of ourselves to meet the needs of others, we, too, are refreshed and renewed by God's grace.

Ultimately, the power of compassion is rooted in God's love for us. Just as He demonstrated the ultimate act of compassion by sending His Son to die for our sins, we are called to reflect that love in our interactions with others. John 3:16 captures this truth: "For God so loved the world, that he gave his only begotten Son, that whosoever believeth in him should not perish, but have everlasting life." This act of sacrificial love is the foundation of our compassion, inspiring us to extend grace, mercy, and kindness to everyone we meet.

As we embrace the power of compassion, may we remember that even the smallest acts of kindness can have a profound impact. Whether it's offering a smile, lending a helping hand, or simply being present with someone in their pain, our compassion reflects the heart of God and brings His light into the world. Let us strive to "be kind one to another, tenderhearted," knowing that our efforts are not in vain and that God is using our compassion to accomplish His purposes. Through His strength, may we continue to embody kindness and empathy, transforming lives and glorifying His name.

Day 24 - Preventing Harm

PREVENTING HARM IS a profound act of love, responsibility, and selflessness, embodying the commandment to "love thy neighbour as thyself" (Mark 12:31). For law enforcement officers, this mission is at the very core of their calling. Each day, they step into situations fraught with uncertainty, risk, and potential danger, not for personal gain but to safeguard the well-being of their communities. They act as shields, stepping into harm's way to protect the vulnerable, to deter wrongdoing, and to ensure safety for others. In every moment of courage, patience, and vigilance, officers demonstrate what it means to love their neighbors through action. Similarly, as followers of Christ, we are called to a life of proactive care, one that prioritizes the safety, dignity, and welfare of those around us. Loving our neighbors is not just a feeling; it is a choice to stand against harm, to intervene where injustice threatens, and to create spaces of peace and protection for all.

For officers, the work of preventing harm begins long before danger arises. It involves training, preparation, and an unwavering commitment to vigilance. They learn to recognize risks, to anticipate threats, and to respond swiftly and effectively to prevent harm before it can unfold. In the same way, as believers, we are called to be vigilant in our relationships and communities, seeking to address the needs of others and to stand as guardians of justice and peace. This might mean stepping in to mediate a conflict, offering support to someone in crisis, or speaking out against actions that could lead to harm. Proverbs 31:8-9 challenges us to "Open thy mouth for the dumb in the cause of all such as are appointed to destruction. Open thy mouth, judge righteously, and plead the cause of the poor and needy." Preventing harm is not passive; it is an active commitment to protecting the vulnerable and advocating for what is right.

Preventing harm also requires empathy—the ability to see the world through the eyes of others and to understand their fears, needs, and struggles. Just as officers approach their work with compassion for those they serve, we are called to respond to others with kindness, patience, and care. Empathy helps us recognize when someone is at risk, whether physically, emotionally, or spiritually, and empowers us to take action. Galatians 6:2 reminds us to "bear ye one another's burdens, and so fulfil the law of Christ." By carrying each other's burdens, we share in the responsibility of preventing harm and promoting well-being in our communities.

At times, preventing harm requires courage. Just as officers face moments of danger to protect others, we may be called to step outside of our comfort zones to stand up for what is right. This might mean confronting harmful behaviors, advocating for those who cannot speak for themselves, or making personal sacrifices to ensure the safety and dignity of others. Joshua 1:9 offers this encouragement: "Have not I commanded thee? Be strong and of a good courage; be not afraid, neither be thou dismayed: for the LORD thy God *is* with thee whithersoever thou goest." This promise reminds us that we do not face these challenges alone; God is with us, equipping us with His strength and guiding us with His wisdom.

Preventing harm also involves fostering environments of peace and safety. Just as officers work to build trust and cooperation within their communities, we are called to create spaces where others feel valued, protected, and cared for. Romans 12:18 exhorts us, "If it be possible, as much as lieth in you, live peaceably with all men." This call to peace requires intentionality—choosing to listen, to understand, and to act with love in our interactions with others. By promoting peace, we help to prevent harm before it begins, creating a foundation of trust and mutual respect that benefits everyone.

At its heart, preventing harm is about reflecting God's love. Jesus's command to love our neighbors as ourselves is not just a guideline for personal relationships; it is a call to action that transforms the way we engage with the world. It challenges us to prioritize the well-being of others, to act with compassion and integrity, and to stand as protectors and advocates for those in need. 1 John 3:18 encourages us, "My little children, let us not love in word, neither in tongue; but in deed and in truth." True love is demonstrated through action, and preventing harm is one of the most tangible ways we can show that love to others.

Preventing harm also requires humility. Just as officers must approach their work with a willingness to learn and grow, we are called to acknowledge our own limitations and to seek God's guidance in our efforts to protect and care for others. Proverbs 3:5-6 reminds us, "Trust in the LORD with all thine heart; and lean not unto thine own understanding. In all thy ways acknowledge him, and he shall direct thy paths." By relying on God's wisdom, we can navigate complex situations with clarity and purpose, ensuring that our actions align with His will.

At times, the work of preventing harm may feel overwhelming or unappreciated. Just as officers face challenges and sacrifices in their efforts to protect others, we may encounter resistance, discouragement, or fatigue in our own efforts to care for our neighbors. Yet, Scripture reminds us that our labor is not in vain and that God sees and values every act of love and service. Galatians 6:9 encourages us, "And let us not be weary in well doing: for in due season we shall reap, if we faint not." By remaining steadfast in our commitment to preventing harm, we reflect God's faithfulness and trust in His promise to bring good from our efforts.

Ultimately, preventing harm is a reflection of God's own character. He is our protector, our refuge, and our shield, watching over us with unwavering love and care. Psalm 121:7-8 assures us, "The LORD shall preserve thee from all evil: he shall preserve thy soul. The LORD shall preserve thy going out and thy coming in from this time forth, and even for evermore." As we strive to protect and care for others, we become instruments of His love, extending His protection and grace to those in need.

May we embrace the call to prevent harm with courage, compassion, and humility, trusting in God's guidance and strength. Let us love our neighbors as ourselves, creating a world where safety, dignity, and peace prevail, and reflecting the heart of Christ in all that we do. Through every act of protection and care, may we glorify God and bring His light to those who need it most.

Day 25 - Provision of Comfort

The provision of comfort is one of the most profound ways we can reflect God's love, offering hope, peace, and reassurance to those in moments of despair, fear, or sorrow. For law enforcement officers, providing comfort is often a hidden but essential part of their role. Whether they are consoling a grieving family, calming a frightened child, or listening to someone overwhelmed by the weight of their circumstances, officers bring a sense of steadiness and compassion to those who feel lost or broken. In these moments, their presence reminds others that they are not alone, that someone cares deeply about their well-being. Similarly, as followers of Christ, we are called to be vessels of comfort, reflecting His boundless love and tender care in our relationships and communities. Isaiah 40:1 declares, "Comfort ye, comfort ye my people, saith your God." reminding us that the provision of comfort is not only a calling but also a divine commission to extend God's heart of compassion to a hurting world.

Comfort begins with presence. Just as officers bring reassurance through their calm and steady demeanor, we are called to be present for others in their times of need, offering a listening ear, a kind word, or simply the gift of our time. In a world that often feels hurried and disconnected, the act of being fully present carries immense power. It tells others that they are valued, that their pain matters, and that they are not alone in their struggles. Romans 12:15 encourages us to "Rejoice with them that do rejoice, and weep with them that weep." This empathy allows us to enter into the joys and sorrows of others, sharing their burdens and reflecting the love of Christ through our presence.

The provision of comfort also involves speaking words of encouragement and hope. Just as officers often find the right words to soothe anxieties or bring clarity in moments of confusion, we are called to speak life and truth into the hearts of those who are hurting. Our words have the power to heal, to uplift, and to remind others of God's promises. Proverbs 16:24 reminds us, "Pleasant words *are as* an honeycomb, sweet to the soul, and health to the bones." By choosing words of kindness, reassurance, and faith, we can bring healing to those who feel weary or broken.

Comfort often requires action. Just as officers step into situations to provide tangible assistance, we are called to meet the needs of others through acts of service and love. Whether it's offering a meal to someone who is struggling, helping a friend navigate a difficult decision, or simply holding a hand during a moment of grief, these actions reflect the heart of Christ and demonstrate His care in practical ways. James 2:15-16 challenges us, "If a brother or sister be naked, and destitute of daily food, And one of you say unto them, Depart in peace, be ye warmed and filled; notwithstanding ye give them not those things which are needful to the body; what doth it profit?" True comfort is more than words; it is a commitment to walk alongside others and to meet their needs in ways that bring relief and hope.

The provision of comfort is not about having all the answers or fixing every problem; it is about being a source of peace in the midst of uncertainty. Just as officers offer a sense of stability in moments of crisis, we are called to point others to the ultimate source of comfort—God Himself. 2 Corinthians 1:3-4 beautifully describes this calling: "Blessed be God, even the Father of our Lord Jesus Christ, the Father of mercies, and the God of all comfort; Who comforteth us in all our tribulation, that we may be able to comfort them which are in any trouble, by the comfort wherewith we ourselves are comforted of God." As we draw from the wellspring of God's comfort in our own lives, we are equipped to share that same comfort with others, becoming conduits of His grace and love.

Comfort also involves patience and understanding. Just as officers approach those in distress with compassion and respect, we are called to be gentle and patient with others as they navigate their pain. Healing takes time, and the journey through grief, fear, or uncertainty is often filled with twists and turns. By walking alongside others with a spirit of patience, we affirm their worth and allow space for God's healing work to unfold. Galatians 6:2 reminds us to "Bear ye one another's burdens, and so fulfil the law of Christ." This act of bearing burdens is not just a practical gesture; it is a sacred calling to share in the struggles of others and to bring the light of Christ into their darkest moments.

The provision of comfort also requires humility. Just as officers must set aside their own emotions or judgments to serve others, we are called to approach those in need with a heart of humility, recognizing that it is not our strength but God's love working through us that brings true comfort.

Philippians 2:3-4 exhorts us, "Let nothing be done through strife or vainglory; but in lowliness of mind let each esteem other better than themselves. Look not every man on his own things, but every man also on the things of others." This humility allows us to serve others selflessly, prioritizing their needs and offering comfort without seeking recognition or reward.

At times, the act of providing comfort may feel overwhelming or even draining. Just as officers face the emotional weight of their work, we may encounter moments when the pain and struggles of others feel too heavy to bear. In these moments, it is essential to turn to God, asking for His strength, guidance, and renewal. Matthew 11:28-30 offers this invitation: "Come unto me, all ye that labour and are heavy laden, and I will give you rest. Take my yoke upon you, and learn of me; for I am meek and lowly in heart: and ye shall find rest unto your souls. For my yoke is easy, and my burden is light." By leaning on God's presence and grace, we are replenished and equipped to continue offering comfort to those in need.

Ultimately, the provision of comfort is a reflection of God's own heart. He is the ultimate Comforter, the One who sees our pain, hears our cries, and meets us in our darkest moments with His unending love. Psalm 34:18 declares, "Come unto me, all ye that labour and are heavy laden, and I will give you rest. Take my yoke upon you, and learn of me; for I am meek and lowly in heart: and ye shall find rest unto your souls. For my yoke is easy, and my burden is light.." As we reflect His compassion and care in our interactions with others, we become instruments of His peace, pointing them to the hope and healing that can only be found in Him.

May we embrace the call to provide comfort with open hearts and willing hands, trusting that God will use our efforts to bring healing, hope, and restoration to those who need it most. Let us be present, speak words of life, and act with love, embodying the spirit of Isaiah 40:1 "Comfort ye, comfort ye my people, saith your God." Through every act of compassion and care, may we glorify God and bring His light to a world in need of comfort and hope.

Day 26 - Protection of the Vulnerable

The protection of the vulnerable is one of the most noble and compassionate acts we can undertake, reflecting the heart of God and His call to defend those who cannot defend themselves. For law enforcement officers, this mission is woven into the fabric of their duty. Every call they respond to, every situation they navigate, and every person they assist is an opportunity to uphold justice and shield the weak from harm. Whether intervening in situations of abuse, protecting children, or standing in the gap for those whose voices are unheard, officers embody the principle of defending the poor and fatherless as commanded in Psalm 82:3: "Defend the poor and fatherless: do justice to the afflicted and needy." Their courage, compassion, and vigilance serve as a reminder of the sacred responsibility we all share to advocate for the vulnerable and to be a force for good in a world that often overlooks those in need.

For officers, protecting the vulnerable requires a combination of strength, empathy, and discernment. They must assess each situation with care, balancing the need for swift action with the importance of understanding the unique needs of those involved. This mirrors the way we, as followers of Christ, are called to engage with those who are struggling or marginalized. Protection starts with awareness—seeing the needs of others and recognizing their value in the eyes of God. It requires us to move beyond our own concerns and to step into the lives of those who are hurting, offering support, advocacy, and love. Proverbs 31:8-9 challenges us, "Open thy mouth for the dumb in the cause of all such as are appointed to destruction. Open thy mouth, judge righteously, and plead the cause of the poor and needy." These words remind us that protecting the vulnerable is not optional; it is a sacred obligation that reflects God's justice and mercy.

Standing up for the weak demands courage. Just as officers face risks and challenges in their efforts to shield others from harm, we are often called to take bold and sometimes uncomfortable steps to defend those who cannot defend themselves. This might mean speaking out against injustice, confronting harmful behaviors, or advocating for change in systems that perpetuate inequality. Isaiah 1:17 urges us, "Learn to do well; seek judgment, relieve the oppressed, judge the fatherless, plead for the widow." These actions require us to put our faith into practice, trusting in God's strength to guide and sustain us as we take a stand for what is right.

The protection of the vulnerable also calls for compassion. Just as officers approach victims of crime or neglect with empathy and care, we are called to respond to the needs of others with tenderness and understanding. This compassion helps us to see beyond the surface, to understand the pain and challenges others are facing, and to offer the kind of support that brings healing and hope. Colossians 3:12 encourages us, "Put on therefore, as the elect of God, holy and beloved, bowels of mercies, kindness, humbleness of mind, meekness, longsuffering." By embodying these qualities, we create an environment where the vulnerable feel valued, respected, and safe.

Protecting the vulnerable also requires perseverance. Just as officers encounter setbacks and resistance in their efforts to bring justice and safety to those in need, we may face obstacles in our own efforts to advocate for others. There will be times when the challenges seem overwhelming or when our efforts appear to yield little fruit. In these moments, it is crucial to remember that our work is not in vain. Galatians 6:9 encourages us, "And let us not be weary in well doing: for in due season we shall reap, if we faint not." By staying faithful to the call to protect and defend, we reflect God's unwavering commitment to justice and His care for the least of these.

At its core, the protection of the vulnerable is an act of love. Jesus's ministry was marked by His compassion for the weak, the sick, and the marginalized. He reached out to those society ignored, offering healing, dignity, and hope. In doing so, He set an example for us to follow, showing us that true strength lies in serving and uplifting others. Matthew 25:40 reminds us, "And the King shall answer and say unto them, Verily I say unto you, Inasmuch as ye have done *it* unto one of the least of these my brethren, ye have done *it* unto me." When we protect the vulnerable, we are not only serving others but also honoring Christ Himself.

Protecting the vulnerable also involves addressing the root causes of harm and injustice. Just as officers work to prevent crime and create safer communities, we are called to engage with the systems and structures that perpetuate inequality or exploitation. This might mean advocating for policies that protect children, supporting organizations that fight human trafficking, or volunteering our time and resources to serve those in need. Micah 6:8 reminds us of this dual calling: "He hath shewed thee, O man, what *is* good; and what doth the LORD require of thee, but to do justly, and to love mercy, and to walk humbly with thy God?" Justice and mercy go hand in hand, and both are essential in our efforts to protect and uplift the vulnerable.

The work of protecting the vulnerable also transforms us. Just as officers find purpose and fulfillment in their efforts to safeguard others, we experience spiritual growth and joy when we step into the role of protector and advocate. Acts of compassion and justice draw us closer to God, allowing His love to flow through us and shaping us into His likeness. Proverbs 11:25 declares, "The liberal soul shall be made fat: and he that watereth shall be watered also himself." By pouring into the lives of others, we find that our own hearts are refreshed and strengthened by God's grace.

Ultimately, the protection of the vulnerable is a reflection of God's own heart. He is the defender of the weak, the champion of the oppressed, and the refuge for those in need. Psalm 68:5-6 describes Him as "A father of the fatherless, and a judge of the widows, is God in his holy habitation. God setteth the solitary in families: he bringeth out those which are bound with chains: but the rebellious dwell in a dry land." As we follow His example, we become His hands and feet in the world, extending His love and justice to those who need it most.

May we embrace the call to protect the vulnerable with courage, compassion, and faith, trusting that God will use our efforts to bring healing, justice, and hope. Let us stand as advocates, defenders, and friends to those who cannot stand for themselves, glorifying God through every act of love and care. Through our actions, may we reflect the truth of Psalm 82:3: "Defend the poor and fatherless: do justice to the afflicted and needy," and bring His light to a world in desperate need of protection and hope.

Day 27 - Perseverance in the Face of Danger

Perseverance in the face of danger is a testament to the strength, courage, and faith that define both law enforcement officers and believers who trust in God's promises. Every day, officers step into situations of uncertainty and risk, armed not only with their training and tools but also with an unshakable resolve to protect and serve. They confront dangers head-on—whether in volatile emergencies, life-threatening scenarios, or the quiet but constant pressure of unpredictability—driven by their commitment to safeguard their communities. Their courage reminds us of a higher calling: to stand strong in the face of life's challenges, drawing on the strength of the Lord to persevere when circumstances feel overwhelming. Joshua 1:9 echoes this call with a resounding promise: "Be strong and of a good courage; be not afraid, neither be thou dismayed: for the LORD thy God is with thee whithersoever thou goest." This verse is not just a command but an assurance that God's presence empowers us to press forward, no matter the dangers or uncertainties we face.

For officers, courage is not the absence of fear but the determination to act despite it. They rely on their training and instincts, yet often must draw on a deeper well of strength to navigate moments of peril. Similarly, in our spiritual lives, perseverance in the face of danger means trusting in God's provision and stepping forward in faith, even when the path is unclear or the obstacles seem insurmountable. This perseverance is rooted in the knowledge that we are not alone—that God walks with us, fights for us, and equips us to overcome whatever challenges we encounter. Isaiah 41:10 reassures us, "Fear thou not; for I am with thee: be not dismayed; for I am thy God: I will strengthen thee; yea, I will help thee; yea, I will uphold thee with the right hand of my righteousness." These words remind us that our courage does not come from our own strength but from the unwavering support of a faithful and loving God.

Perseverance also requires a deep sense of purpose. Just as officers are driven by their mission to protect and serve, we are called to live with purpose, aligning our actions with God's will and trusting that He is working through us. When faced with dangers—whether physical, emotional, or spiritual—our perseverance is fueled by the understanding that our struggles are not meaningless but are part of a larger story of redemption and victory. Romans

8:28 affirms this truth: "And we know that all things work together for good to them that love God, to them who are the called according to his purpose." By keeping our eyes fixed on God's plan, we can endure hardships with hope, knowing that He is using our perseverance to shape us, strengthen us, and bring glory to His name.

In the face of danger, perseverance also requires faith in God's promises. Just as officers rely on their trust in their team and training, we must lean on the promises of Scripture to sustain us. God's Word is a source of encouragement and strength, reminding us of His faithfulness and giving us the courage to press on. Psalm 27:1 declares, "The LORD is my light and my salvation; whom shall I fear? The LORD is the strength of my life; of whom shall I be afraid?" This confidence in God's power and presence allows us to face even the most daunting challenges with peace and assurance.

At times, perseverance in the face of danger requires us to step out of our comfort zones and take risks for the sake of others. Just as officers willingly put themselves in harm's way to protect the vulnerable, we are called to sacrifice our own safety or comfort to stand up for what is right, to defend those in need, and to be a light in the darkness. John 15:13 reminds us of the ultimate act of courage and love: "Greater love hath no man than this, that a man lay down his life for his friends." While we may not always be called to such extreme sacrifices, this verse challenges us to live selflessly, putting the needs of others above our own and trusting God to guide and protect us.

Perseverance also involves resilience in the face of setbacks and failures. Just as officers must recover quickly from mistakes or unexpected outcomes, we are called to rise again after every stumble, trusting in God's grace to sustain us. Proverbs 24:16 offers this encouragement: "For a just man falleth seven times, and riseth up again." This resilience is born of faith, a confidence that God's strength is made perfect in our weakness and that His plans for us remain steadfast, even when we falter. By leaning on His grace, we can press on with renewed determination, knowing that He is at work in every moment.

The courage to persevere is not something we muster on our own; it is a gift from God, cultivated through prayer, faith, and reliance on His Spirit. Just as officers prepare for the dangers they face by honing their skills and maintaining their readiness, we prepare for life's challenges by staying rooted in God's Word, seeking His presence in prayer, and building a community of support. Ephesians 6:10-11 exhorts us, "Finally, my brethren, be strong in the Lord, and in the power of his might. Put on the whole armour of God, that ye may be able to stand against the wiles of the devil." By equipping ourselves with God's truth and power, we are ready to face whatever comes our way, confident in His ability to protect and sustain us.

Perseverance in the face of danger also brings opportunities for growth and transformation. Just as officers develop greater skill, confidence, and resilience through their experiences, we, too, are shaped by the trials we endure. James 1:2-4 encourages us to embrace these moments as opportunities for growth: "My brethren, count it all joy when ye fall into divers temptations; knowing this, that the trying of your faith worketh patience. But let patience have her perfect work, that ye may be perfect and entire, wanting nothing." Through perseverance, we become stronger, more faithful, and more aligned with God's purposes, reflecting His glory in every aspect of our lives.

Ultimately, perseverance in the face of danger is a reflection of God's character. He is the ultimate example of steadfastness, never wavering in His love for us, His commitment to our salvation, or His faithfulness to His promises. As we persevere, we become more like Him, embodying His strength, courage, and compassion in a world that desperately needs His light. 1 Corinthians 15:58 calls us to this steadfastness: "Therefore, my beloved brethren, be ye steadfast, unmovable, always abounding in the work of the Lord, forasmuch as ye know that your labour is not in vain in the Lord." This assurance gives us the courage to press on, knowing that our perseverance is part of God's eternal plan.

May we, like the officers who face danger with courage and resolve, embrace the call to persevere in the face of life's challenges, trusting in God's strength and promises to guide us. Let us be strong and of good courage, knowing that the Lord our God is with us wherever we go, equipping us to overcome every obstacle and to stand firm in His truth and love. Through every trial, may our perseverance bring glory to His name and draw us closer to the fullness of His purpose for our lives.

Day 28 - Power of God's Word

The power of God's Word is unmatched, serving as our ultimate authority, guide, and source of strength in every circumstance. Just as law enforcement officers rely on laws to uphold justice, maintain order, and ensure fairness, we as believers rely on the Word of God to direct our lives, shape our decisions, and align our hearts with His truth. Hebrews 4:12 declares, "For the word of God is quick, and powerful, and sharper than any twoedged sword, piercing even to the dividing asunder of soul and spirit, and of the joints and marrow, and is a discerner of the thoughts and intents of the heart." This verse captures the living and active nature of Scripture, reminding us that God's Word is not merely a set of rules or ancient writings but a dynamic force that penetrates the deepest parts of our being, transforming us from the inside out.

For officers, laws provide a framework for their work, offering clarity and authority in their pursuit of justice. In a similar way, God's Word offers believers a foundation upon which to build their lives, providing guidance, comfort, and correction in a world often marked by confusion and uncertainty. The Bible is our roadmap, showing us how to live in alignment with God's will and revealing His character, promises, and purpose for our lives. Psalm 119:105 proclaims, "Thy word is a lamp unto my feet, and a light unto my path." Just as a lamp illuminates the way in darkness, Scripture sheds light on our journey, guiding us through the challenges, decisions, and uncertainties we face.

The power of God's Word lies in its ability to reveal truth and expose falsehood. Just as officers rely on laws to discern right from wrong, we rely on Scripture to distinguish between God's ways and the world's ways. It serves as a mirror, reflecting our true selves and showing us where we fall short, while also offering hope through the promise of grace and redemption. James 1:22-25 encourages us to not only hear the Word but to act upon it: "But be ye doers of the word, and not hearers only, deceiving your own selves. For if any be a hearer of the word, and not a doer, he is like unto a man beholding his natural face in a glass: For he beholdeth himself, and goeth his way, and straightway forgetteth what manner of man he was. But whoso looketh into the perfect law of liberty, and continueth therein, he being not a forgetful hearer, but a doer of the work, this man shall be blessed in his deed." Living out God's Word transforms us into people who not only know His truth but embody it in our actions and attitudes.

Scripture is also our greatest weapon in spiritual battles. Just as officers equip themselves with tools to enforce the law and protect others, we are called to wield the sword of the Spirit, which is the Word of God. Ephesians 6:17 places Scripture as part of the armor of God, emphasizing its role in defending against the lies, temptations, and attacks of the enemy. Jesus Himself demonstrated the power of God's Word when He resisted Satan's temptations in the wilderness, responding to each attack with the authority of Scripture: "It is written..." (Matthew 4:4-10). This example reminds us that God's Word is not only a source of guidance but also a weapon of truth and victory, enabling us to stand firm in faith and resist the forces that seek to pull us away from Him.

The power of God's Word extends beyond guidance and protection; it also has the ability to comfort and heal. Just as officers offer reassurance and support to those in distress, Scripture speaks peace into our hearts when we feel overwhelmed, anxious, or broken. Psalm 34:18 offers this promise: "The LORD is nigh unto them that are of a broken heart; and saveth such as be of a contrite spirit." In times of sorrow or struggle, God's Word reminds us of His presence, His love, and His faithfulness, providing a source of hope that sustains us through even the darkest valleys.

God's Word is also the foundation of our faith. It reveals His plan of salvation, His promises to His people, and His unchanging character. Through Scripture, we come to know the depth of His love, the extent of His grace, and the certainty of His sovereignty. Romans 10:17 states, "So then faith cometh by hearing, and hearing by the word of God." By immersing ourselves in Scripture, we deepen our trust in God and strengthen our ability to live out our faith with boldness and conviction.

Moreover, the Word of God equips us for every good work. Just as officers study and apply the law to carry out their duties effectively, we are called to study and apply Scripture in our daily lives, allowing it to shape our thoughts, words, and actions. 2 Timothy 3:16-17 affirms the all-encompassing nature of God's Word: "All scripture is given by inspiration of God, and is profitable for doctrine, for reproof, for correction, for instruction in righteousness: That the man of God may be perfect, throughly furnished unto all good works." Scripture not only teaches us what is right but also prepares us to live out our calling as followers of Christ, equipping us to serve, lead, and love others in His name.

The transformative power of God's Word is evident not only in individual lives but also in communities and nations. Just as laws bring order and justice to society, Scripture has the power to bring about reconciliation, healing, and restoration on a larger scale. When individuals and communities align themselves with God's Word, they reflect His kingdom on earth, creating environments of love, peace, and justice. Isaiah 55:11 captures the unstoppable nature of God's Word: "So shall my word be that goeth forth out of my mouth: it shall not return unto me void, but it shall accomplish that which I please, and it shall prosper in the thing whereto I sent it." This assurance reminds us that Scripture is not just informative but transformative, achieving God's purposes wherever it is proclaimed.

Ultimately, the power of God's Word lies in its ability to connect us to the heart of God. It is His love letter to humanity, His blueprint for abundant life, and His invitation to a relationship with Him. Through Scripture, we hear His voice, understand His will, and experience His presence in a deeply personal way. John 1:1-3 reveals the divine nature of God's Word: "In the beginning was the Word, and the Word was with God, and the Word was God. The same was in the beginning with God. All things were made by him; and without him was not any thing made that was made." This passage reminds us that God's Word is not separate from Him but an integral expression of His being, a reflection of His wisdom, and the foundation of all creation.

As we rely on the power of God's Word, may we approach it with reverence, humility, and a desire to be transformed. Let us immerse ourselves in its truths, allowing it to shape our minds, strengthen our faith, and guide our steps. Just as officers depend on laws to carry out their mission, may we depend on Scripture as our ultimate authority, trusting in its power to lead us, protect us, and draw us closer to the One who speaks through it. Through the living and active Word of God, may we experience the fullness of His grace, the depth of His love, and the unshakable hope that sustains us in every season of life.

Day 29 - Putting Others First

Putting others first is an act of profound humility, love, and sacrifice, reflecting the heart of Christ and the call to serve selflessly. For law enforcement officers, this principle is evident in their daily commitment to prioritize the safety and well-being of others above their own. Whether responding to emergencies, protecting the vulnerable, or standing in harm's way to ensure the safety of their communities, officers embody the spirit of putting others first. Their courage and dedication remind us of a higher calling—to live not for ourselves but to uplift, protect, and serve those around us. Philippians 2:3 captures this beautifully: "Let nothing be done through strife or vainglory; but in lowliness of mind let each esteem other better than themselves." This verse challenges us to let go of pride, to value others above ourselves, and to reflect God's selfless love in all we do.

For officers, putting others first often means making difficult decisions, enduring long hours, and facing personal risk to ensure the safety and peace of their communities. It requires a heart of compassion and a willingness to sacrifice comfort, time, and even personal desires for the greater good. Similarly, as believers, we are called to adopt this posture of humility and service in our relationships, families, and communities. Putting others first means seeking their well-being above our own, prioritizing their needs, and acting with a spirit of generosity and love. Matthew 20:26-28 reminds us of this call: "Whosoever will be great among you, let him be your minister; And whosoever will be chief among you, let him be your servant: Even as the Son of man came not to be ministered unto, but to minister, and to give his life a ransom for many." Jesus Himself is the ultimate example of selflessness, showing us that true greatness is found in serving others with humility and love.

Putting others first requires intentionality. Just as officers approach their work with a sense of duty and purpose, we must approach our interactions with a commitment to prioritize the needs of others. This might mean listening with patience when someone is struggling, offering help without expecting anything in return, or choosing kindness over convenience. Galatians 6:2 encourages us, "Bear ye one another's burdens, and so fulfil the law of Christ." By sharing in the struggles and challenges of others, we demonstrate the love of Christ and create a culture of care and support.

At its core, putting others first is about reflecting the character of Christ. Jesus's entire ministry was marked by selflessness, as He healed the sick, fed the hungry, and ultimately gave His life for the salvation of humanity. His love was not conditional or selective; it was a love that sought to uplift, restore, and serve all who came to Him. As His followers, we are called to embody this same love, letting go of selfish ambitions and embracing a life of service. John 13:14-15 captures this call: "If I then, your Lord and Master, have washed your feet; ye also ought to wash one another's feet. For I have given you an example, that ye should do as I have done to you." Washing feet was an act of humility and care, and Jesus's example reminds us that no act of service is too small or insignificant when done in love.

Putting others first also involves recognizing the value and dignity of every person. Just as officers serve individuals from all walks of life, we are called to see each person as a child of God, worthy of respect and compassion. This perspective transforms our interactions, allowing us to approach others with kindness, patience, and grace. Romans 12:10 encourages us, "Be kindly affectioned one to another with brotherly love; in honour preferring one another." By honoring others, we reflect God's love and create an environment where everyone feels valued and supported.

However, putting others first is not always easy. Just as officers face challenges and sacrifices in their work, we may encounter moments when selflessness feels difficult or costly. There will be times when prioritizing others requires us to set aside our own desires, endure inconvenience, or give more than we feel we can. Yet, Scripture reminds us that these sacrifices are not in vain. Hebrews 13:16 encourages us, "But to do good and to communicate forget not: for with such sacrifices God is well pleased." Every act of selflessness is an offering to God, a reflection of His love, and a testimony to His grace.

The act of putting others first also brings joy and fulfillment. Just as officers find purpose and satisfaction in serving their communities, we experience a deeper sense of peace and joy when we live selflessly. Acts 20:35 reminds us of this truth: "It is more blessed to give than to receive." By prioritizing the needs of others, we discover the richness of a life lived for others, a life that mirrors the heart of Christ and brings glory to His name.

Putting others first is not about neglecting our own needs but about trusting God to provide for us as we care for others. Just as officers rely on their training, teams, and resources to fulfill their duties, we rely on God's strength and provision to sustain us in our acts of service. Matthew 6:33 encourages us to seek God's kingdom first, trusting that He will meet our needs: "But seek ye first the kingdom of God, and his righteousness; and all these things shall be added unto you." By placing our trust in Him, we are free to serve selflessly, knowing that He is faithful to care for us in every way.

Ultimately, putting others first is a reflection of God's own heart. He is the ultimate example of selflessness, giving His only Son so that we might have eternal life. John 3:16 declares, "For God so loved the world, that he gave his only begotten Son, that whosoever believeth in him should not perish, but have everlasting life." This sacrificial love is the foundation of our faith and the model for how we are called to love and serve others.

May we embrace the call to put others first with humility, courage, and faith, trusting that God will use our efforts to bring hope, healing, and joy to those around us. Let us "esteem other better than themselves," reflecting the love of Christ in every act of service and creating a world that shines with His light and grace. Through our selflessness, may we glorify God and draw others closer to Him, living as His hands and feet in a world that desperately needs His love.

Day 30 - Presence of God in Every Situation

The presence of God in every situation is a promise of unwavering support, unmatched strength, and unshakable peace that sustains us through every challenge, triumph, and moment of uncertainty. Just as law enforcement officers stand ready to respond, protect, and serve their communities at all times, God is always with us, watching over us, walking beside us, and providing everything we need. His promise in Hebrews 13:5, "I will never leave thee, nor forsake thee," is a powerful reminder that we are never alone. No matter the circumstance, whether we are facing joy or sorrow, calm or chaos, God's presence is constant, a steady anchor that holds us firm and reminds us of His unfailing love.

For officers, their readiness to act provides reassurance to those they serve, a sense of security in times of fear or crisis. In the same way, God's presence gives us the confidence to face life's challenges, knowing that we are not left to navigate them on our own. His presence brings comfort in the midst of grief, courage in the face of fear, and strength when our own reserves are depleted. Psalm 46:1 declares, "God is our refuge and strength, a very present help in trouble." These words remind us that God is not distant or detached; He is actively involved in our lives, offering us refuge and empowering us to endure whatever comes our way.

The presence of God is not confined to moments of crisis; it permeates every aspect of our lives. Just as officers are present in both visible and unseen ways, working behind the scenes to maintain order and safety, God's presence is constant, whether we are aware of it or not. He is with us in the ordinary and the extraordinary, in moments of celebration and moments of sorrow. Deuteronomy 31:8 reassures us, "And the LORD, he it is that doth go before thee; he will be with thee, he will not fail thee, neither forsake thee: fear not, neither be dismayed." This promise reminds us that God goes ahead of us, preparing the way and ensuring that His plans for us are fulfilled.

God's presence provides strength when we feel weak and weary. Just as officers draw strength from their training, their teams, and their mission, we draw strength from the knowledge that God is with us, equipping us to face each day with courage and faith. Isaiah 40:29-31 offers this encouragement:

"He giveth power to the faint; and to them that have no might he increaseth strength. Even the youths shall faint and be weary, and the young men shall utterly fall: But they that wait upon the LORD shall renew their strength; they shall mount up with wings as eagles; they shall run, and not be weary; and they shall walk, and not faint." When we rely on God's presence, we find a source of strength that transcends our human limitations, enabling us to persevere and thrive even in the face of adversity.

The presence of God also brings peace that surpasses understanding. Just as officers work to bring calm and order to chaotic situations, God's presence quiets the storms in our hearts, replacing anxiety with trust and fear with confidence. Philippians 4:6-7 encourages us, "Be careful for nothing; but in every thing by prayer and supplication with thanksgiving let your requests be made known unto God. And the peace of God, which passeth all understanding, shall keep your hearts and minds through Christ Jesus." This peace is not dependent on our circumstances; it flows from the assurance that God is with us, that He is in control, and that His plans for us are good.

God's presence also guides us, providing wisdom and direction when we feel uncertain or lost. Just as officers rely on their training and experience to navigate complex situations, we rely on God's Word and His Spirit to lead us in the right path. Psalm 32:8 promises, "I will instruct thee and teach thee in the way which thou shalt go: I will guide thee with mine eye." Through prayer, Scripture, and the quiet nudges of the Holy Spirit, God illuminates our path, helping us to make decisions that align with His will and purpose.

The presence of God is a source of joy and hope. Just as officers inspire confidence and reassurance through their dedication and service, God's presence fills our hearts with a joy that cannot be shaken by the trials of life. Psalm 16:11 declares, "Thou wilt shew me the path of life: in thy presence is fulness of joy; at thy right hand there are pleasures for evermore." This joy is not fleeting or superficial; it is a deep and abiding sense of contentment that comes from knowing we are loved, valued, and never alone.

God's presence is also a reminder of His faithfulness. Just as officers remain committed to their duty regardless of the challenges they face, God's presence is steadfast and unchanging. He is with us in every season of life, from the mountaintops to the valleys, from moments of triumph to moments of doubt. Lamentations 3:22-23 proclaims, "It is of the LORD's mercies that we are not consumed, because his compassions fail not. They are new every morning: great is thy faithfulness." This faithfulness assures us that God's presence is not contingent on our circumstances or our performance; it is a reflection of His unchanging nature and His boundless love for us.

Through God's presence, we find the courage to face life's challenges with confidence and hope. Just as officers rely on their training and their team, we rely on the presence of God to sustain us, to equip us, and to remind us that we are never alone. Whether we are walking through moments of joy or moments of trial, His promise to never leave us or forsake us is a source of unshakable strength and peace.

May we live each day with the awareness of God's presence, drawing strength from His promises and trusting in His unfailing love. Let us face life's challenges with courage and faith, knowing that the God who stands with us is greater than any obstacle we may encounter. Through His presence, may we find peace, joy, and hope, and may we glorify Him in all that we do, confident that He is with us always.

Day 31 - Praise for God's Faithfulness

Praise for God's faithfulness is a song that echoes through the hearts of all who have experienced His unchanging love, unwavering support, and steadfast presence. Just as law enforcement officers serve faithfully, committing themselves daily to protect and care for their communities despite challenges, dangers, and sacrifices, we are called to celebrate and rely on the infinite faithfulness of our God. His faithfulness is a foundation that never wavers, a promise that never falters, and a truth that sustains us through every moment of life. Lamentations 3:23 beautifully declares, "Great is thy faithfulness," reminding us that God's mercies are new every morning, and His love for us endures without fail. This is not just a poetic phrase—it is the bedrock of our hope, a truth that carries us through seasons of triumph and trial, joy and sorrow, and everything in between.

For officers, faithfulness is a commitment that goes beyond duty. It is the consistent choice to show up, to serve with integrity, and to persevere even when the path is hard. Similarly, God's faithfulness is the unchanging nature of His character—His promise to never leave us, to fulfill His Word, and to work all things for good in our lives. His faithfulness is evident in the rising sun, in the unfolding of His plans, and in the countless ways He provides for, protects, and loves His people. Psalm 36:5 captures this truth: "Thy mercy, O LORD, is in the heavens; and thy faithfulness reacheth unto the clouds." This imagery reminds us that God's faithfulness is limitless, extending beyond what we can comprehend or imagine.

God's faithfulness is a source of strength in times of uncertainty. Just as officers face unpredictable challenges with resolve, we can face life's uncertainties with confidence, knowing that God's faithfulness never changes. He is the same yesterday, today, and forever (Hebrews 13:8), and His promises are as true now as they were thousands of years ago. When we are weary, He is our strength; when we are afraid, He is our refuge; when we feel lost, He is our guide. Isaiah 41:10 offers this reassurance: "Fear thou not; for I am with thee: be not dismayed; for I am thy God: I will strengthen thee; yea, I will help thee; yea, I will uphold thee with the right hand of my righteousness." In every trial, God's faithfulness is a constant presence, a steady hand that holds us firm.

The faithfulness of God is not dependent on our circumstances or our actions. Just as officers remain committed to their duty regardless of the challenges they face, God's faithfulness is unchanging, rooted in His character rather than our performance. Even when we falter, He remains steadfast. 2 Timothy 2:13 reminds us, "If we believe not, yet he abideth faithful: he cannot deny himself." This truth is a profound comfort, assuring us that God's love and promises are not conditional—they are anchored in His perfect and unchanging nature.

God's faithfulness is a source of provision. Just as officers ensure the safety and well-being of their communities, God meets every need of His people with perfect timing and care. He provides strength for the weary, peace for the anxious, and hope for the brokenhearted. Philippians 4:19 promises, "But my God shall supply all your need according to his riches in glory by Christ Jesus." This provision is not limited to material needs; it encompasses every aspect of our lives, from the deepest desires of our hearts to the smallest details of our days. His faithfulness ensures that we are never lacking, for He is the Good Shepherd who cares for His flock with love and devotion.

The faithfulness of God invites us to respond with praise and gratitude. Just as communities honor the faithful service of officers, we are called to honor and glorify God for His unchanging love and mercy. Psalm 100:4-5 exhorts us, "Enter into his gates with thanksgiving, and into his courts with praise: be thankful unto him, and bless his name. For the LORD is good; his mercy is everlasting; and his truth endureth to all generations." Praise is not just an expression of thanks; it is an act of trust, a declaration that we believe in His goodness and faithfulness even when life feels uncertain or difficult.

God's faithfulness also gives us hope for the future. Just as officers remain committed to building safer, stronger communities, God's faithfulness assures us that His plans for us are good and that His promises will be fulfilled. Jeremiah 29:11 declares, "For I know the thoughts that I think toward you, saith the LORD, thoughts of peace, and not of evil, to give you an expected end." This hope anchors our souls, reminding us that God is in control and that His faithfulness will carry us through every season of life.

Through God's faithfulness, we find the courage to persevere. Just as officers demonstrate resilience and resolve in the face of challenges, we are empowered by the knowledge that God is with us, guiding us and strengthening us for the journey. Galatians 6:9 encourages us, "And let us not be weary in well doing: for in due season we shall reap, if we faint not." By relying on God's faithfulness, we can press on with confidence, knowing that our efforts are not in vain and that His promises will come to pass.

Ultimately, God's faithfulness is a reflection of His love. It is the foundation of our relationship with Him, the assurance that we are never alone, and the guarantee that His plans for us are good. Romans 8:38-39 captures this truth with beautiful clarity: "For I am persuaded, that neither death, nor life, nor angels, nor principalities, nor powers, nor things present, nor things to come, nor height, nor depth, nor any other creature, shall be able to separate us from the love of God, which is in Christ Jesus our Lord." This love, expressed through His faithfulness, is a source of endless comfort, strength, and joy.

May we live each day with hearts full of praise for God's faithfulness, trusting in His promises and celebrating His unchanging love. Let us, like officers who serve with steadfast commitment, honor Him with our lives, reflecting His faithfulness in our actions, words, and relationships. Through every trial and triumph, may we declare with confidence and joy, "Great is thy faithfulness," and find peace in the knowledge that His mercies are new every morning and His love endures forever.

Conclusion

As we conclude "Hearts of Valor - Faithful in the Call", we pause to reflect on the journey we've walked together through these 31 days. This devotional was designed not just as a momentary source of encouragement, but as a foundation for an enduring connection to the God who calls, equips, and sustains each of you in your noble service. Every verse, every reflection, every prayer has been an invitation to lean into the unshakable truth that you are never alone in your call to serve and protect. Law enforcement is a profession of unparalleled courage and dedication, but it is also one that demands strength, resilience, and faith that can only come from the One who stands with you in every moment. The closing of this devotional does not signal an end but rather a beginning—a call to carry forward the truths you have embraced, the encouragement you have received, and the strength you have found into every aspect of your life and work.

Your calling as a law enforcement officer is more than a job; it is a mission, a divine appointment to be a guardian of justice, a defender of the vulnerable, and a beacon of hope in a world often overshadowed by darkness. It is a mission that requires you to rise above fear, fatigue, and uncertainty, knowing that the One who has called you is faithful to complete the good work He has begun in you (Philippians 1:6). Each day brings new challenges—some expected, others completely unforeseen—but in every shift, every call, every moment of uncertainty, you have the assurance of God's presence. He promises, "I will never leave thee, nor forsake thee" (Hebrews 13:5). This is the anchor that holds you steady, the foundation that keeps you grounded, and the truth that empowers you to walk boldly into the unknown.

As you continue in your role, remember that faithfulness is not about perfection; it is about persistence. It is about showing up, day after day, with a heart that is willing, even when the path feels difficult or the load feels heavy. It is about trusting that God's strength is made perfect in your weakness (2 Corinthians 12:9) and that His grace is sufficient for every challenge you face. Let the truths you have explored in this devotional be a wellspring of encouragement when the demands of your work weigh on your spirit. Let the reminders of God's faithfulness, love, and provision be the fuel that keeps your heart steadfast and your steps firm, even in the face of adversity.

To continue faithfully in your call, you must remain rooted in God's Word. Scripture is your ultimate guide, your source of wisdom, and your defense against the pressures and challenges of this world. Just as you rely on your training and experience to navigate complex situations, rely on the Word of God to direct your heart, renew your mind, and equip you for every good work (2 Timothy 3:16-17). Make time to dwell in His presence, to pray without ceasing (1 Thessalonians 5:17), and to seek His guidance in all things. These spiritual disciplines are not just practices; they are lifelines that connect you to the strength, wisdom, and peace of God. In your moments of doubt or weariness, remember that His Word is a lamp to your feet and a light to your path (Psalm 119:105), illuminating the way forward when the road feels uncertain.

Never underestimate the power of prayer as you continue in your journey. Prayer is not only a means of seeking God's help but also a way of drawing closer to His heart and aligning your will with His. It is in prayer that you find the courage to face the dangers of your role, the peace to handle the stress, and the compassion to serve with humility and grace. Bring every burden, every fear, every victory, and every decision to God in prayer, trusting that He hears you and will answer in His perfect way and time. As Philippians 4:6-7 reminds us, "Be careful for nothing; but in every thing by prayer and supplication with thanksgiving let your requests be made known unto God. And the peace of God, which passeth all understanding, shall keep your hearts and minds through Christ Jesus."

In the face of the unique pressures and challenges of law enforcement, community is essential. Surround yourself with people who will encourage you, pray for you, and remind you of God's faithfulness when your spirit feels weary. Whether it's fellow officers, family, friends, or a church community, lean on the support of those who share your values and will walk alongside you in faith. Proverbs 27:17 reminds us, "Iron sharpeneth iron; so a man sharpeneth the countenance of his friend." Together, you can spur one another on to good works, holding each other accountable and celebrating the victories, big and small.

Lastly, let your life be a testimony to the God who called you. The way you serve, the way you love, and the way you persevere in the face of challenges is a reflection of His grace and power at work in you. As you protect and serve your community, remember that you are also representing the Kingdom of God, shining His light in places that desperately need hope and healing. Matthew 5:16 encourages us, "Let your light so shine before men, that they may see your good works, and glorify your Father which is in heaven." Through your faithfulness, your integrity, and your compassion, you have the opportunity to point others to the ultimate source of justice, peace, and redemption.

"Hearts of Valor - Faithful in the Call" is not just a devotional; it is a declaration that you are part of a greater story, one written by a God who loves you, equips you, and walks with you every step of the way. As you close these pages, may you carry the truths within them into every aspect of your life, continuing to serve with courage, humility, and unwavering faith. May you find strength in God's promises, peace in His presence, and joy in the knowledge that your work is not in vain. Take heart, for you are never alone; the God who called you is faithful, and He will sustain you as you remain faithful in the call.

Don't miss out!

Visit the website below and you can sign up to receive emails whenever Joshua Rhoades publishes a new book. There's no charge and no obligation.

https://books2read.com/r/B-A-AJLBB-MUZIF

BOOKS 2 READ

Connecting independent readers to independent writers.

Did you love *Hearts of Valor - Faithful in the Call*? Then you should read *Why It Matters- Finding Hope in Moments of Frustration*[1] by Joshua Rhoades!

Welcome to a journey of hope and healing in the face of life's most challenging moments. "Why It Matters: Finding Hope in Moments of Frustration" speaks directly to those who have felt the relentless waves of life's struggles—those who know the pain of pouring themselves into something only to watch it unravel. It's for the hearts that have cried out, "Why, God?" while staring down paths that feel endless and unyielding. If you've ever questioned whether your pain has a purpose or if your struggle is seen, this book was written with you in mind.

In the raw and unfiltered spaces of discouragement and doubt, this book offers a light. It's a guide for navigating the heavy moments when hope seems like a distant whisper amid life's storms. Through Scripture "Why It Matters" invites you to uncover the sacredness in your struggles and the deeper meaning within your frustration. This isn't just a story about enduring hardship—it's a roadmap to discovering God's hand in your most vulnerable seasons.

---

1. https://books2read.com/u/md9E9l

2. https://books2read.com/u/md9E9l

This book explores how God uses our frustrations to refine us, build resilience, and draw us closer to Him. Through the lives of biblical figures, you'll see that you're not alone in feeling stuck or overwhelmed. Each chapter reveals how God doesn't waste our pain but instead weaves it into a tapestry of redemption, growth, and grace. Every tear, every moment of waiting, and every prayer uttered in desperation becomes a building block for something greater.

You'll be reminded that even when progress feels slow or nonexistent, God is at work. He is present in every moment, writing a story of hope and restoration. Each trial you face isn't just a hurdle to overcome—it's an opportunity for transformation and deeper faith.

This book isn't merely a collection of words; it's an invitation. It's a call to journey through the places where faith is tested and hope feels faint. Together, we'll find that God's purposes are present in every frustration, and we'll see the beauty of His plan, even when it's hidden in the shadows of life's hardest days.

So, if you're ready to rediscover the hope that lies beyond frustration, to lean into the truth that God is working even in the mess, and to embrace the possibility that your struggles are shaping something meaningful, let's begin. There's hope waiting on the other side of your pain. Let's find it together.